MY
Lozells
FAMILY

MY Lozells FAMILY

Ordinary Lives, Extraordinary People

GILL MANSELL

BREWIN BOOKS

BREWIN BOOKS
19 Enfield Ind. Estate,
Redditch,
Worcestershire,
B97 6BY
www.brewinbooks.com

Published by Brewin Books 2021

A CIP catalogue record for this book is
available from the British Library.

ISBN: 978-1-85858-741-7

Printed and bound in Great Britain
by Dig Print.

Contents

For my grandchildren Norah, Liliana and Jude
because my family history is their history too.

Lozells? Where's that?

This is the usual response I get when as a Brummie (now living in the Black Country); I get asked which part of Birmingham I come from. Few people seem to have heard of it (apart from the infamous race riots in 1985) but when I say it's between Handsworth and Aston, they can usually locate it. But for me, Gillian Hewitt, as a child born in 1949 and brought up in Lozells, it was my world and it never occurred to me that it was not the biggest and best area in the whole of Birmingham!

But where did it all begin? Why the name 'Lozells'? I always thought as a child that the name 'Lozells' was unusual but it was not until I was an adult that I discovered that the name came either from a term used in Middle English during the 14th century which derives from the verb 'to lose' or from a 19th century term meaning 'rogue or scoundrel', neither explanation is a good advert for the area!

We were very proud of our local 'stately home' Aston Hall. This is a Grade 1 Jacobean house built by Sir Thomas Holte between 1618 and 1635. The Holte stand at nearby Villa Park football ground is a reminder of this local history. In 1643 Aston Hall was besieged by the Parliamentary forces during the English Civil War and the great oak staircase still bears the scars of this bombardment. It is surrounded by Aston Park but it does not have the same ambience now as they built a motorway next to it but it is still worth a visit. Lozells Wood was originally the common pasture of Aston Manor or Hall in the Middle Ages where local peasants had the right to graze their livestock. The area remained mainly rural and there was a farm and a nursery in the area in the early 1800s – hence we still have Farm Street and Nursery Road.

With the coming of the Industrial Revolution and Birmingham being at the forefront and close to the jewellery quarter, Lozells began to change and grow from about 1830 and Birmingham became known as the 'city of a thousand trades'. Matthew Boulton built his big house and factory manufacturing steam engines at Soho and the water for the factory came from Hockley Brook. As a child, looking over the brick wall at Hockley Brook in Farm Street, I would not have thought that such a little insignificant trickle of water had been so important in the Industrial Revolution! The only local trade I remember was the Hooks pearl button factory in Villa Street. The popularity of pearl buttons grew in the Victorian and Edwardian era and Hooks was one of a number of such factories. My school friend Sandra lived on the other side of Church Street and her garden backed onto the factory in Villa Street. We used to dig about in her garden and find mollusc shells with some pearl still inside them, they seemed like treasures to us.

By 1860, good quality houses for workers were built in the area and it became a residential location for the people who worked in the local trades. The district was not included in the 1960 adjacent redevelopment of Newtown so some of the houses still remain, including the house I was brought up in.

For such a small area, there were a lot of churches and schools. The local Wesleyan church on Villa Road had a football team which eventually became Aston Villa Football Club. There was St Silas church in St Silas Square off Church Street, St Paul's on the Lozells Road, the Salvation Army in Nursery Road to name just a few. On Hunters Road, a convent was built opposite the St Francis Catholic Church, it was designed in 1840 by the architect AW Pugin, the famous architect who also designed the Houses of Parliament and Big Ben. It was the first Roman Catholic religious house to be built in the area since the Reformation.

But to us, as children, Lozells was just our playground. The edge of that playground was Lozells Road at the top and Nursery Road at the bottom. Beyond the bottom of Nursery Road was Hockley and so was 'out of area'. The side borders were Villa Street and Burbury Street, beyond these lay the unknown.

Lozells is more than just an area you go through to get from Aston to Handsworth or vice versa or a place with some interesting history. My family lived in the area for several generations and my mother had a fund of stories about her parents, in-laws and life in Lozells from the beginning of the 20th century.

Today, my parents and grandparents' lives seem like an alien world totally unrelated to life today. They led ordinary lives but they were extraordinary people, living in hard times, but carrying on and dealing with whatever life brought their way. It would be a pity to lose such a wealth of information from the 'old days', stories of humour, sadness and all the other emotions which made up the tapestry of family life in Lozells from the early 20th century. So here is our family story and the story of Lozells; the two are very much intertwined.

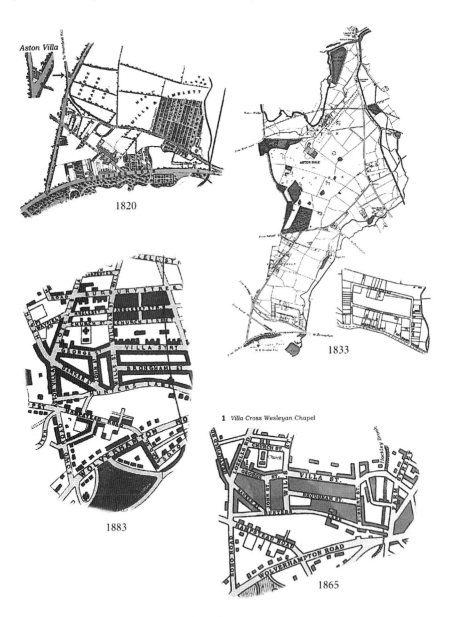

Church Street.

Great grandpa Johnson.

Great grandmother Jemima with her granddaughter Constance.

The Johnson Family.

Chapter 1

My Grandparents

THE JOHNSONS

My mother's parents were Minnie and Harry Johnson and they lived at a rented house, 193 Burbury Street, Lozells. Neither of them were very tall – about 5ft 2" – and they used to address one another as 'Mick' but no-one knows why. Their early upbringing was quite different.

Grandpa Johnson – Harry – early life

Grandpa Harry Johnson was born on 28 March 1890 and came from what could be classed as a lower middle class family who lived in Summer Row; they owned a newsagents shop. His mother's name was Jemima Grimmett. It was said that Grandpa Johnson's father also used to be part time chauffeur for the Lord Mayor of Birmingham, Neville Chamberlain, so when Nan and Grandpa got married on 31 July 1915, they had use of the mayoral carriage. The Johnsons must have been fairly well off financially because Nan had a beautiful engagement ring – diamond shaped made up of diamonds which must have cost a pretty penny in those days. Grandpa Johnson's occupation on the marriage certificate was toolmaker so he was on reserved occupation and not in the Army.

Harry had two sisters, May and Jemima and two brothers, Thomas and Ralph. We don't know a lot about Uncle Ralph, Mom described him as 'a lady's man'; he died young in 1918, unmarried. I have a photo of him, a dark haired handsome looking gentleman, smartly dressed, sitting on a bench, a bit of a mystery man.

In his younger 'politically incorrect' days, Harry used to do an Al Jolson impersonation. Al Jolson was an American singer of sentimental ballads such

Uncle Ralph – the ladies man.

as 'Swannee', 'Mammy' and 'Climb upon my knee, sonny boy' and used to 'black up', a theatrical genre from the 19th century. Al Jolson was called the world's greatest entertainer and starred in one of the first 'talkie' films, The Jazz Singer. I have a photo of Grandpa 'blacked up' in his Al Jolson costume.

At some point in Harry's early life, he was looking for work and walked to Coventry and back to see if he could get a job – a distance of 40 miles. But men would go anywhere if there was a prospect of work and wages; there was no unemployment or sickness benefit then. There was no NHS either and you had to pay to see a doctor, some people used to pay 2 pence a week into a scheme to enable you to see one.

Grandpa Johnson had very dark curly hair and used Morgan's Pomade to keep it under control, this was a hair darkener a bit like Brylcreem. The Morgan Pomade Company was founded in 1873 and is the oldest independent manufacturer of hair and beauty products in England – it is still going. But to Nan, this gooey stuff was a nightmare as it left Grandpa's pillows with a yellow imprint which was hard to remove in the wash. He also used to take snuff; he used to put a pinch of snuff up each nostril and then give an almighty sneeze and he always left traces of snuff on his suit jacket. Keeping him presentable was a full time job. He had a gold fob watch and chain which

Grandpa Johnson
impersonating Al Jolson.

A young nanny Johnson
with the racing pigeons.

he wore in his 'wescott' (waistcoat). We still have this watch in the family; it was passed down to my brother, being the only grandson in the Johnson family and will continue to be passed onto the eldest sons.

When we were young, Grandpa used to listen to 'The Archers' (an everyday story of country folk) on the radio and if we visited whilst this was on, we had to keep silent until the programme finished. If he had a cup of tea, he would never drink it from the cup, he used to tip the tea into the saucer and drink from it with a loud slurping sound.

He also kept homing pigeons which were housed in a large wooden aviary in the yard opposite the back door. He later went on to keep budgies.

Their home

This was a terraced house in Burbury Street and the front door opened directly onto the street; there was no front garden. It had a front room which had the 'best' furniture, heavy Victorian style; it was only used as a way through to the middle living room. The front room had a small dark passageway leading into the middle living room which was also small and crammed with furniture. There was a huge sideboard with a back on it with a mirror but it had lots of exciting cupboards and drawers in it. Nan used to let my brother and my cousins 'mooch' in the drawers to see if we could find anything exciting, such as odd buttons, or bits of material. The stairs to the bedrooms were behind a door in the middle living room. There was one large bedroom overlooking the front and another two bedrooms to the rear. I remember these rear bedrooms as being almost empty, because as soon as my mother and her sister were married, Nan sold the contents of their rooms! There was a scullery type kitchen with a big white sink which was used for everything – laundry, washing vegetables, personal hygiene to name but a few. Then you went outside to the toilet and the dustbin hole beyond the scullery. There was a yard and a blue brick path which led to the back gate. The gate opened onto an alleyway at the back of the houses which came out in Graham Street. There was a small garden either side of the path but the garden was only really used as a way out of the back. My grandparents never had a bathroom and the first time my grandpa had a proper bath was when he went into hospital with a burst duodenal ulcer in his 70s.

In the dark passageway between the front and living room was the cellar door on the right and another cupboard opposite where the coats were kept. This door had coat hooks on the inside and when it swung open, Nan's fox fur would swing out from behind the door, head and eyes and all, and frighten us.

Nan wearing her 'scary' fox fur.

Nanny Johnson – Minnie – early life

My nan, Minnie Elizabeth Dean was born on 21 May 1891. Her family by contrast to her husband's were poor. Her mother, Minnie Palmer, was born on 30 October 1867 and George Dean, her father, was born around 1866. Nan's mom and dad married on 30 October 1887 and lived in Ford Street, Hockley. Nan's dad's occupation on his marriage certificate was 'brass burnisher' and men who did this type of work often ended up with lung problems as there were no protective face masks in those days. He died in a sanatorium in his 40s. She had a sister Mabel, and brothers Harold and Cyril. Harold was in the army during World War 1 but Cyril was too young. Nan's mother did not go to her wedding stating that Nan was too young to marry (she was 24) but it may have been because she could not afford the clothing for herself; Mabel was a bridesmaid and 'the babby' Cyril is on the wedding photo proudly wearing a suit with an Eton collar shirt.

Nan was a good singer when she was a girl and used to sing in the church choir. She used to sing music hall songs to us when we were little and she used to bounce us on her knee as she sang 'Here Comes the Galloping Major'. She had beautiful long hair and kept it long all her life, wearing it in a bun as she got older. She left school at the age of 12 and worked in a pawn shop 100 hours a week for little money. She said that women would come into the pawn

Wedding of Nan and Grandpa Johnson 1915.

shop on a Monday morning bringing in their husband's one and only suit to pawn and sometimes brought in the sheets, still warm off the bed to pawn. One of her jobs was to check the bedding and clothing for fleas and ticks! The women used to reclaim their goods on Fridays when their husbands got paid. This was a weekly ritual.

Johnson family life

My Aunty Connie was born in 1916 but my mother was not born until 1922. It seems that Nan had a miscarriage in 1918. This was all summed up in one sentence by Mom, "Nan had a boy called Geoffrey who she lost on the 'po' when the maroons went off". Maroons were a type of rocket which made a loud noise and smoke and were used when German bombers were approaching. Up to 1917, the Germans used airships to drop bombs so you usually had plenty of time to shelter when you saw an airship approaching. From 1917, the Germans used planes to bomb the country so an early warning defence system was required and this was the maroons. Presumably, Nan must have been shocked at the explosion and gave premature birth on the 'po' or potty. This life changing event, summed up in one sentence, was typical of the age. Early death was something which was not unusual as it happened to everyone around you; death was part of the warp and woof of life.

When young, Nan had signed 'the pledge' with the Band of Hope. This was an organisation set up by Anne Carlile in 1847 in Leeds to discourage drinking. Anne was convinced that children suffered because of the ready availability of strong drink for their parents. She met a young Baptist minister, Jabez Tunnicliff who had experienced a dying alcoholic who clutched at his sleeve and made him promise to warn children about the dangers of drink. They joined forces and at its height, the Band of Hope numbered 3.5 million children and adults and Queen Victoria was its Jubilee patron. The pledge they signed was "that I may be my best and give my best in service, God help me, I will abstain from all alcoholic drinks".

It was well known that men used to get paid on a Friday and go to the pub and spend it; some wives used to wait outside the pub to get money off their husbands before they went in. From the beginning of their marriage, Grandpa used to like to go for a drink with his old mates in Aston so Nan used to 'dog' him to see what he was up to. Christmas was the worst time and even when older, Mom used to hate Christmas as it reminded her of her childhood. Grandpa would come home drunk and in a bad mood on Christmas Eve and once kicked the dining table up in the air. Another time, he threw his coins onto the open fire and Nan had to scrabble around in the ashes to retrieve them. In the end, Nan gave up 'the pledge' and went with him to the pub, their regular pub being the Waterloo in Wills Street, or The Angel on the corner of Wills Street and George Street if they wanted a change. They used to go every lunchtime and every evening. I also remember Nan sending me to the 'outdoor', a few doors down from where she lived, to get a jug of beer for them. My nan liked to drink sherry with an egg in it at home. I asked to try it when I was a girl and it was horrible, the egg wasn't mixed properly and it was like drinking slime.

Mom was named Marguerite after the daughter of Grandpa's brother Thomas who had emigrated to Rhode Island USA. She was never called by her proper name though. Grandpa used to breed dogs and his favourite dog was one called Molly, so Mom became 'Molly' for the rest of her life. Nan used to keep rabbits which Mom used to look after as pets. But Nan used to then kill them and make rabbit stew and Mom remembered sitting crying at the dinner table as Nan used to try to make her eat it. She also used the rabbit fur to make gloves and I remember having a pair of rabbit backed fur gloves when

I was a little girl. Grandpa also kept chickens which he used to kill and eat. As a small child Mom actually saw a headless chicken running round their back yard. He kept pigeons and finally he bred budgies and so we always had to have a budgie. The one I remember the most, we called Torchy from the TV programme, Torchy the Battery Boy.

Nan and Grandpa used to take Mom and her sister on holiday, usually to Aberystwyth when young and Mom had a hand knitted swimsuit. This was great until you came out of the sea – it had stretched so much, the neck was somewhere round your waist. They continued to go until her sister Connie and her boyfriend Ben and Mom and Dad were courting and even after they were married. Uncle Ben used to call

Grandpa Johnson with his favourite dog Molly.

it 'Aberwristwatch'. Mom remembers being in a café on the front at Aberystwyth when there was a violent thunderstorm. A flash of lightning struck the telephone on the inside wall of the café, blew it off the wall and the waitress fainted.

Mom had an older sister, Constance Edna and to look at them, you would not know they were sisters. Mom had very curly blonde hair and Connie had dark hair. Connie was born on 4 August 1916 and both she and Mom lived at home until they were married. Aunty Connie was married on 5 July 1941 to Reginald Eric Benbow (always known as Ben) and she had to walk to the church on her wedding day as the taxis had been bombed out. The wedding reception

Ben, Connie, Mom and
Dad in Aberystwyth.

Mom on the left, Nanny Johnson in the middle, Connie on the right.

Connie and Ben's wedding.

was at home and they had to move all the food quickly off the dining table to underneath the table as there was an air raid during the reception.

Grandpa Johnson loved to go fishing and when he was younger, he had a motorbike and sidecar to take the family with him. He kept the maggots in a tin on a shelf in the kitchen and once when Mom was given stew for dinner, there was a maggot in it. Nan simply fished it out and told her not to be so fussy. One of Grandpa's fishing haunts was Lapworth canal and once when he was fishing on his own, he dozed off and fell into the canal. He traipsed off to the nearest pub and the landlord lent him a pair of trousers to go home in. The only problem was that the landlord was about 6ft and Grandpa was about 5ft 2" so the turn ups on the trousers were up to his knees!

He and Nan sometimes used to go on the bus to Lapworth and take the fishing tackle with them. Once when sitting on the bus, Nan noticed that the man sitting in front of her had maggots crawling around the brim of his hat. The lid had come off their 'National Dried Milk' tin containing the maggots on the overhead luggage rack and the contents of it were busy doing a lap of honour around the passenger's hat.

Nanny Johnson was fairly strict with Mom and her sister and Mom remembered having to come home from school in her lunch break on Monday to help Nan with the washing in the tiny scullery. This was done in a large galvanised tub and the washing pounded with a 'maid' or wooden podger and

Mom with her dad fishing.

then put through the wringer by hand. I sometimes used to help my nan with this and when we were putting sheets through, often water got trapped in the sheets and it sprayed out as it went through soaking us.

Mom had a chest illness, empyema, when she was young and had a chance to go to Switzerland to recuperate with a scheme set up by a local newspaper. Nan would not let her go because she could not go with her. Mom also passed for grammar school but could not go because her parents could not afford the uniform and books necessary. She passed instead to go to the British School of Commerce in Birmingham to learn secretarial skills. She was awarded £4 10 shillings but I doubt she saw any of this!

When Mom was courting, she used to have to wash up after Sunday lunch before she was allowed to go out and remembers standing at the sink in her best 'costume', a two piece suit and hat washing the pans as quickly as she could to get out on time. Nan used to open Mom's post even when she was older and if Mom said anything to her she used to say "I'm your mother, I've a right to know". She applied this rule to everything until Mom got married and left home. She used to have all Mom's weekly wages off her and give her half a crown (2 shillings and 6 pence) for herself out of which she had to clothe herself, buy stockings and make up but half a crown didn't really go very far.

Mom aged 17.

Grandpa Johnson was also strict with Mom and her sister Connie. Mom started work at 14 in the offices at Joseph Lucas, Hockley. She had long blonde very curly hair which was much admired. Her mom used to brush her hair when she was young and it was so thick, it used to get tangled. If she wriggled, Nan used to 'clonk' her on the head with the back of the hairbrush to get her to sit still. When she got to 17, she wanted it cut as it was quite difficult to maintain but Grandpa forbade her. Eventually with Nan's compliance, she went to have it cut and the hairdresser gave her back her cut hair in a brown paper parcel. She took it home to Grandpa who immediately threw the parcel on the fire and held it down with a poker. He did not speak to her for weeks.

Before Mom was married, she and Nan used to like to go to a Saturday afternoon tea dance but Grandpa was not too happy about them going so they used to hide their dance shoes in the outside toilet and collect them on their way out to the back gate. Nan used to embarrass Mom at these dances by seizing hold of available men and saying 'Ere, she'll dance with ya!' Mom also once decided to improve her front contour by wearing 'falsies', pads you put inside your bra. Unfortunately, she discovered at the end of the dance that one of the 'falsies' had worked its way round to her back. This was not the contour she was hoping to achieve!

My nan believed that you should never go outside without wearing a hat as you would catch 'your death'. As their toilet was outside, she used to hang a hand-knitted beret on the back of the kitchen door to wear to go to the toilet. She used to call the dustbin 'the midden' and remembered the night soil men coming to empty the 'midden' during the night. She lived next door to her neighbour, Mrs Davies, for many years but they always addressed each other as 'Mrs...' never by their Christian names. She also used to warn us about crossing the 'hoss road' and to never go out with wet hair as you would catch pneumonia. Nan always wore a beret, summer as well as winter and she had her dresses made by a local seamstress. She used to buy a bolt of fabric, usually a flowery pattern and the dresses were always made to the same pattern, round neck and long sleeves; I never saw her with bare arms. Nan and Grandpa wore 'comms' or combinations as undergarments. They were like the thermal leggings of today and these too were worn all the year round. Nan's comms came to just below her knees so when she sat down, her comms were visible; I thought she had her knees bandaged!

We usually went round to Nanny Johnson's every day after school, Mom used to call it 'clocking in with your Nan'. We used to get a cup of tea; it was weak and made with sterilised milk. There were no teabags then, only loose tea leaves, these were supposed to be strained out when the tea was poured. Nan was not too fussy about this and there were always tea leaves left at the bottom of the cup. I used to leave the last bit of tea as I hated the tea leaves; I still do not drink a complete cup of tea, a hangover from tealeaf avoidance. My brother used to drain the cup and was sometimes seen sporting a tea leaf stuck between his teeth.

The remembrance of poverty stayed with Nan all her life and although Grandpa had a good job at Lucas's and a pension, she was careful about money. Grandpa used to give her 'housekeeping'; money which was the norm in those days. When he was older, he loved to have gorgonzola cheese and mussels every week and Nan used to charge him extra for these items. She used to keep a list of her household expenses and I have a copy of one from 1953. The week after Mom got married, Nan sold her bed, Mom said jokingly it was to stop her from going home again. But marriage then was very much a case of "You've made your bed, so lie in it" whatever the circumstances. Divorced women were regarded with suspicion... they were to be kept at arm's length away from anyone's husband.

When they were older, Nan and Grandpa liked to go to a matinee performance at the Theatre Royal, Aston. They also used to go to the Lucas Sports and Social Club on Hockley Hill. This was an enormous brick building and was for anyone who worked at Lucas's. There was a dance floor and Nan and Grandpa used to like to go on a Saturday night to trip the light fantastic. Mom and Dad used to go with them sometimes as they liked dancing.

As Grandpa got older, he mellowed and I only remember him as a sentimental person who cried when you gave him birthday or Christmas presents. When he was happy, he used to say 'Well, I'm in my oil tot'. This saying came about because in his youth, men thought that if they drank a tot of olive oil before they had a drink – or two it would prevent them from getting drunk. Suffice to say, it didn't work.

Nan and Grandpa Johnson on their Golden Wedding Anniversary.

THE HEWITTS

Early life Grandpa Hewitt – Ernest

I know very little about Grandpa Hewitt's background. He was born on 27 June 1881 and a relative of mine researching the family tree discovered that his father came from Sheffield but apart from that fact, he is a mystery. His parents may have come to Birmingham looking for work as Grandpa was born in Birmingham.

Early Life – Nanny Hewitt – Kate Eden

Kate was one of six sisters; there was Hilda, Priscilla, Dorothy, Alice and Nellie. She was born on 24 April 1884. Her parents were Charles Eden and Catherine Dudley; Charles Eden, Nan's father was born on 2 October 1856 and I have the original copy of his birth certificate. Charles Eden's father was listed as a journeyman. This meant he was either someone who had finished his apprenticeship in a trade or could be just another name for an employee. On Nan's wedding certificate, his occupation is shown as 'jeweller'. Charles's mother is listed as a pearl button maker but she was unable to write her name so 'made her mark' on his birth certificate.

Nan married in St Saviour's church, Hockley on 4 June 1906 and Grandpa Hewitt's occupation is listed as an 'engraver' which meant he was in the jewellery trade. Nan and Grandpa stayed at home and lived with her parents. Nan was born and died in the same house. I remember her as a tallish thin woman with her hair in a hairnet; I have no idea if her hair was long or short. She was a very good cook and made cakes and wonderful pastry pies. She was also the one you went to if you were ill. She used to make a poultice for your neck when you had a sore throat. This was made by boiling onions and while they were still warm, stuffing them into a man's sock to wear around your neck. For chest complaints, you had a mustard plaster. This was made by

The Eden family.

mixing flour, mustard powder and warm water and putting it between two pieces of material eg a tea towel or old sheet and applying it to the chest. It was meant to sweat out all the 'badness' but you had to be careful it was not too hot, or you would end up with blisters.

Dad described his mother as 'a most unhappy woman' and I do not remember her smiling much. She was a woman of few words and she certainly did not wear her heart on her sleeve. The only clue we ever got for her unhappiness was when Mom's first baby died. Mom went to tell her he had died and all she said was, pointing at Grandpa, 'why couldn't it have been him, he's no use to anybody'. Maybe she was simply disappointed that things hadn't worked out as she would have liked them to but she was stoical and just got on with things as you did in those days.

On Mom and Dad's wedding photo, she is giving a faint smile but Mom said that she didn't like losing Dad because he was 'the goose that laid the golden egg' at number 134. Every week, from the moment he got married, Dad used to give his mom some money as they did not have a lot. It caused some friction between Mom and Dad as Mom resented the fact that Dad's parents smoked and drank whisky which she did not consider a good use of money. Mom had to keep the same winter coat for years when we were young but Dad still insisted on giving money weekly to his parents.

Mom and Dad wedding group photo.

Family Life

My father's parents, Kate and Ernest Hewitt lived at the bottom of Church Street at number 134 and Dad was born in the house. He had two older sisters, Alice and Kitty, but being a bit of a late arrival and a boy, he was everyone's pet, including his Aunt Hilda, Nan's sister who still lived at the house. Hilda

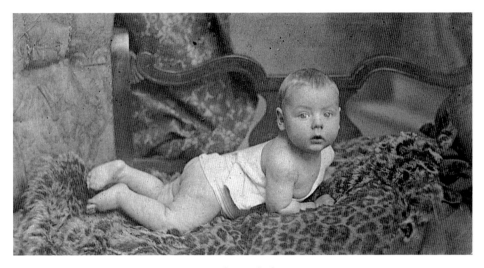

Dad as a baby.

Dad aged 2.

A young Aunty Hilda.

was born on 22 April 1900 and was a tall no-nonsense woman who did not mind speaking her mind and did not suffer fools gladly. There is a photo of her as a child and her expression then sums her up. She worked at Greys in Bull Street in Birmingham; she worked in the haberdashery department. She also worked part time as a bar maid in The Vine pub in Villa Street. She did not marry until her 50s and it came as a bit of a shock. Grandpa Hewitt made one of his surreptitious visits to our house and announced 'Our Hilda's getting married!'. Through working at The Vine, she had met Alf McGrann, he had been married twice before, once divorced and once widowed. They seemed an unlikely pair because Alf was very short compared with Hilda but she was very proud of 'little Alfie'. The first family party he came to, at Nanny Hewitt's, some of the men were a bit the worse for wear and were considering whether to stop there overnight. Discussing sleeping arrangements, Grandpa Hewitt came up with 'And you can get in with the budgie, Alf'. I don't know how everyone managed to keep their faces straight. Alf worked in the jewellery trade at home and for all the ladies in the Hewitt family, he made enamelled brooches of budgies and they were very well done. Grandpa Hewitt had his own view on the partnership, he was a shrewd judge of character – 'He'll soon

Hilda and Alf's wedding.

Christmas card from a young Dad to relatives.

have her back at work' and he was right. Hilda asked Dad to give her away at the wedding and after she and Alf were married, they lived in Carpenters Road and little Alfie gave up work as he had emphysema through smoking; Hilda went back to work at Greys. Aunty Hilda gave up smoking to help Alf give up and they managed for a while. Eventually Alf said 'If I can't smoke, I may as well die'. So he started smoking again and later died from emphysema. Aunty Hilda had a soft spot for Dad and when she was widowed, Dad continued to look after her until she died in 1981.

Grandpa Hewitt had been in the Oxford & Bucks Light Infantry in World War 1 and was injured. He had been shot in the left forearm near Ypres and so had a war pension. He developed angina in his early 40s and in those days, it was considered so serious, he never worked again. The household also included Dad's grandparents. Later on, when the grandparents had died, they also had what they called a 'PG' – a paying guest, not a lodger! His name was Ernest Howard but we called him Mr Howard, I think he was an old army pal of Grandpa's. He worked in an office and he wore a brown pin stripe three piece suit. So now there were three Ernest's in the house – father, son and PG. Mr Howard used to sit at the table to eat his meal in the breakfast room and ate off a tin army plate. I can still hear the loud scraping noise he made whilst he ate his tea and when we visited, we usually had to wait until he had finished his noisy meal before we could hear what other people were saying. There was a small scullery type kitchen. This had a leather strop, like a belt, hanging up by the sink for Grandpa Hewitt to sharpen his cutthroat razor on. There was a breakfast room, another room with a piano and a front room which was for best and never used; I don't recall ever going into this room or being allowed upstairs. There was a big grandfather clock in the hall which was very decorative but purely ornamental – the chimes were missing. The front door was

Great Grandpa Eden with Dad.

never used, I can't remember it ever being open, we always went down the entry through the back gate to the back door.

When Dad's grandpa was ill in bed, my dad as a lad used to go upstairs to see him and roller skate around the bedroom. Grandpa Hewitt used to send Dad out to place his secret bets at an illegal bookies at the back of someone's house. Gambling was not made legal until 1960 so sending a young lad out to do this would not arouse suspicion. Deliveries in those days were made by horse and cart, not only milk deliveries but also goods such as salt. This came in blocks and the local supplier was Dick the 'salt man'. If a horse and cart came down Church Street, Grandpa used to send Dad out with a shovel after the horse to collect the manure to put on the rhubarb he grew in the garden. Dad went to Anglesey Street school, the school playground was at the bottom of his garden.

Dad was keen on trainspotting as a boy and while he was still young, his mom used to give him a halfpenny bus fare to go unaccompanied to Snow Hill station for trainspotting. He was also allowed to take his bike to bits on the mat in front of the fire in the breakfast room. When he was younger, Dad rode a bike (he did not learn to drive until he was 46) and had two accidents on his bike. Once his wheels got stuck in the tram lines on the Soho Road, Handsworth and he fell off and broke his thigh bone. The second accident also involved tram lines – he got stuck in them at Aston Cross and fell off and broke his collar bone. When he was courting Mom, he also once went swimming in the pool at Sutton Park and caught some sort of lung disease which involved a stay in hospital.

Prior to Grandpa Hewitt having angina he had worked in the jewellery quarter as did Nanny Hewitt's family. My grandmother left me a lovely gold

Dad age 7 at school, front row, middle.

Grandpa Hewitt in later years.

locket which had been hers and it was beautifully engraved on the outside and was not heart shaped, but hexagonal. Although Mom said Nanny Hewitt was a 'cold' woman, inside the locket was a photo of Mom with Rex, the baby who died and a small blond curl. She may not have shown it, but her feelings ran deep. She also left me a half gold sovereign probably because I was the only granddaughter on the Hewitt side. My cousins were Bobby, Alan and Chris who were older than me and there was my brother, Stephen. As I was growing up, I remember my grandparents sitting in arm chairs side by side in the breakfast room, both smoking Park Drive like a pair of chimneys, Nan once set her chair on fire by accident.

As children, we used to see them regularly and Nan was a great knitter. She used to knit jumpers for me, I remember she once knitted me a lilac short sleeved jumper with a purple cardigan... very classy. The only problem was that Mom had to wash all the knitted stuff before I could wear it as it reeked of cigarette smoke.

Dad was a dutiful son to his parents all their lives. Grandpa Hewitt was always laid back. He used to say to us children 'If you don't behave, I am going to jump on your eyebrows!' When the family used to talk in front of him in the house, they must have forgotten he was there. If there was anything of interest to be repeated, he used to come up to our house, I can remember him coming through the back gate and beckoning to my mom through the living room window, 'Ere, I've got something to tell ya'. There were no secrets in the Hewitt household because we used to get to hear about everything from Grandpa Hewitt. When the news finally came out, Mom had to pretend it was a surprise.

My two sets of grandparents were very different, but as children we saw them regularly. We used to go to the Hewitt's regularly and sit in the breakfast room opposite Nan and Grandpa in their chairs. There was a large Singer sewing machine on the opposite wall and we used to sit in chairs either end of this. Nan always had some cake she had made and Grandpa used to take the plates off us, sometimes before we had finished, to wash up. Sometimes Dad's sister Aunty Kitty came as well and when we all used to leave together, Aunty Kitty used to stop off at our house to discuss the family news before she went home to number 76. In later years, Aunty Alice and Uncle Les used to take Nan and Grandpa Hewitt on holiday every year in their caravan. It was only a small caravan and they all smoked so the atmosphere must have been rather heavy!

But seeing grandparents frequently was usual in the days when I was a child as everyone lived so close and it would be unthinkable to pass by their houses without going in. Grandpa Johnson died in 1976 and Nan reluctantly continued

Grandpa and Nanny Hewitt with Les.

to live on her own in Burbury Street. Later on she developed dementia and had to move to a home in Aston; she died there age 94. Grandpa Hewitt died in 1965 age 84 from a heart attack and Nanny Hewitt died on 21 November 1967 age 83 from a kidney problem. They were all very much part of our young lives and I look back on all my grandparents with affection. I am grateful for their involvement in our lives and for all I learned from them about life.

*Grandpa and Nanny Hewitt
with me in the middle.*

*Stephen, Grandpa Johnson
and me in our garden.*

Mom with her dad on holiday.

Mom on left, Connie on right.

May with baby Eileen.

Front row: Jane and May with Eileen in the middle. Back row: Jane's husband, Arthur, on the left and May's husband, Frank, on the right.

Mom age 10½.

Dad in his first car.

Nan and Grandpa Hewitt in their garden.

Mom on holiday.

Chapter 2

The Extended Family

My Dad was born at 134 Church Street and moved up to 100 Church Street after marrying Mom. One of his sisters, my Aunty Kitty and Uncle Harry lived at 76 Church Street. My nan, Mom's mom, lived at 193 Burbury Street and Mom's sister, Aunty Connie and Uncle Ben and my cousins, Diane and Lynn, lived at 194 Burbury Street. My Aunty Cis lived in Lozells Street, my Aunty Alice and Uncle Dan lived in Carpenters Road. When my Aunty Hilda married later in life, she moved from 134 Church Street to Carpenters Road. We did not have to travel very far to see our relatives and even at a young age, we would go on our own to see them.

THE HEWITTS

Dad's eldest sister, Alice married Leslie Bignell and she went to live in Kings Norton where a new housing estate had been built in what was once a rural area. When Mom and Dad were courting, they used to go on the bus to see Alice and her two sons, Bobby and Alan, while Les was away in the war. Alice was quite a laid back person and once when Mom and Dad were visiting her, they were having a chat when Alan, one of her lads (who Alice called Ally bally) climbed onto the sideboard in his boots and cut a picture out of a frame with a knife; Alice did not turn a hair or when Alan pushed Bobby out of the front window and broke his arm. When Les returned from the war, I think that the regime changed!

Dad's other sister, Kitty (Kate) lived at 76 Church Street and was married to Harry Leather who had been a neighbour of the Hewitt family. Dad remembers old Mrs Leather having a sort of dementia when she got older

Alice and Les's wedding 1934.

Kitty and Harry's wedding 1934.

and she would often go missing. They used to send Dad out, being a young lad, to find her; he usually did find her – down at the pub!

Aunty Kitty was always smartly dressed and her husband Uncle Harry regularly wore a trilby hat when he went out; he used to doff his hat to you as he went by. He too worked in the jewellery trade at H Samuels in Hunters Road and would walk down Church Street to work every day. I sometimes used to go up to Aunty Kitty's on a Sunday morning when she was making pastry. She would let me help and even though my pastry frequently ended up on the kitchen floor, she still used to bake it for me even though it was slightly dirty.

Aunty Kitty had one son, Christopher who was 10 years older than me, and I was bridesmaid at the age of 10 at his wedding to Barbara. The two older bridesmaids had dresses in a nasturtium orange colour and I had a white dress with a nasturtium orange sash and satin sandals dyed to match. We had no car in those days so after the wedding I had to go to the wedding reception on the bus still dressed in my finery. We went back to Aunty Kitty's after the reception and as usual they set up a 'bar' in the breakfast room. This was two upturned beer crates with a plank across. Whilst everyone was occupied, we didn't notice my brother Stephen, who was six at the time, playing 'barman'

Uncle Harry with Stephen. *Aunty Kitty with a young Chris.*

Me, second left, as a bridesmaid at Chris and Barbara's wedding.

by pouring all the remains of glasses into one glass and drinking it. Good job he was caught before any real harm was done.

Nanny Hewitt had five sisters. Hilda lived with her until she got married. Aunty Alice married Uncle Dando and lived in Carpenters Road, they had no children and she died at a relatively young age. Aunty Cis lived in Lozells Street and her husband, Charlie, died before I was born. She could not have children so she took on a baby girl who she called Gwen. Gwen was being offered by a barge family or bargees with a lot of children who could not afford to feed another one. Barge families or 'bargees' travelled up and down the canals in Birmingham carrying goods and coal. Once this had been a lucrative business but when the railways arrived, they lost a lot of business so they became quite poor. Travelling about, they did not always get to register the birth of their children and did not appear on any censuses. Thus it was relatively easy to arrange a 'private' transaction if they had another baby they could not afford to feed. It was not until the 1950s that this adoption was formalised. It was arranged by Uncle Les because as a Clerk of the Court in Birmingham, he could arrange for a solicitor to legalise the process.

Nanny Hewitt's other two sisters were Dorothy and Nellie, they emigrated to Canada in the early 1920s under an immigration scheme and settled in

Aunty Nellie's visit from Canada.

Toronto. I nearly did not come into being because Nellie and Dorothy wanted to take Dad with them but Nan would not let him go. Aunty Nellie came back for a visit when I was about eight and there is a family photo of us all in Nanny Hewitt's garden – the house had been Nellie's childhood home. When Mom and Dad were in their 80s, there was a knock on the door and there was Bill, Dorothy's son from Canada, and Dad's cousin. He had been doing some research on his family history but when he went to find number 134, it wasn't

there as it had been demolished to make way for the Anglesey Street school extension. He thought he would try to find out where Dad had moved to but fortunately for Bill, he hadn't moved. Bill looked very similar to Dad, the Eden connection was definitely there. Mom and Dad took him to the Black Country Museum and he was fascinated by the houses there as the interiors were exactly the same as his mother would have lived in.

Cousin Bill on the left, Dad on the right.

A Christmas family party.

Most family parties were held at the Hewitt's, I don't remember going to Nanny Johnson's for a party. Although they did not have a lot of money, the food was always good and plentiful. We used go to Nanny Hewitt's every Christmas for dinner because she said that it may be the last year Grandpa would be with us; he had angina in his forties and hadn't worked since... he lived till his eighties! Mom had a saying for people who were always on the point of dying but managed to hang on – 'a creaking gate swings the longest'. It was certainly true in Grandpa Hewitt's case. There were always turkey sandwiches, pickles, trifle and a cake. There was also beer available and one year, the uncles became so drunk, they started to drink the pickled onion vinegar. Needless to say, they were all very ill the next day. There was always a sing song; Grandpa Hewitt's party pieces were war songs 'Mademoiselle from Armentieres' this was popular in the First World War. The only part I recall was joining in at the end of the song with 'Inky Pinky Parley Voo'. He also used to sing 'Lili Marlene', popular in the Second World War. And there was always a rousing chorus of 'Let's All Go Down the Strand, have a banana'. Grandpa Hewitt also displayed his talent for 'playing the spoons' which was a way of banging two spoons together on your knee and with your hand to produce a rhythm. He tried to teach me how to do this but I never quite got the knack.

Nan's sister, Aunty Cis (Priscilla) lived in Lozells Street and Mom used to take us to visit her. She made the most amazing jam tarts and I was always hopeful that she had been baking when we went.

We also went to parties at Aunty Cis's at Christmas. Aunty Cis was a rather large lady with a huge bosom which was covered in a 'pinny' (pinafore). She was good at nursing babies and used to say 'put them on my feather pillow (bosom) and I will get them to sleep'. It always worked.

At Aunty Cis's parties, we used to play a horse racing game, Escalado, betting our halfpennies and pennies, and the grown-ups used to get very heated during the race and very loud. My uncle Cyril, Aunty Gwen's husband, in particular, had a very sharp loud voice which used to frighten me and I used to hide under the table. We also used to play a card game called 'Newmarket' and we children were sometimes given halfpennies to play. The Boxing Day parties were either at Nanny Hewitt's or at her sisters, Aunty Cis in Lozells Street but the format was the same wherever we were. One Boxing Day, at Aunty Cis's, we were in the middle room and her grandson and his wife were in the front room with the wife in the process of giving birth (she had a daughter) but nothing stopped a good party.

THE JOHNSONS

Grandpa Johnson had a sister Jane Eliza, called Jinny and her main claim to fame in the family was that as a young girl, she had a mass of curly hair and it had once got stuck on the flypaper. This was a strip of very sweet sticky paper hanging from the ceiling which they used to attract flies to keep them away from the food. Her hair was so strongly attached that they had to cut a piece of her hair off to remove her from the flypaper. She married Uncle Arthur but he died young and they had no children. She lived in Wellhead Lane, Perry Barr and when we were young, she had a sweet shop there and we used to go and visit her, there seemed to be cats everywhere!

Aunty Jinny with her curly hair.

Jane, Harry's sister and her husband Arthur.

May Johnson, Harry's sister.

Frank Howes, May's husband, a policeman.

Aunty Eileen.

Aunty Hazel.

Grandpa Johnson's other sister, May also lived in Wellhead Lane. She had married Uncle Frank, a policeman, who also died young. She had two daughters, Eileen and Hazel, neither of whom married. Aunty Eileen was once engaged but it was said in the family that Aunt May and Hazel disapproved so the engagement was broken off. Nan said it was doomed from the moment Eileen had a pearl engagement ring because pearls are for tears! Aunty Hazel, in particular, could 'talk the hind legs off a donkey' and all we had to do was listen! Aunty Eileen worked for British Gas and used to play cricket in one of

Aunty Eileen with her fiancé.

their teams. Their house in Wellhead Lane was immaculately tidy and Aunty May had a glass china cabinet absolutely choc-a-bloc with tiny knick-knacks

Eileen playing cricket.

Mabel Dean.

Hazel with May.

Eileen with May.

which we were allowed to look at but not touch; Aunty Hazel cleaned them every day. They all had to move from Wellhead Lane when their house was demolished to make way for Birmingham City University and they moved to a much more modern house in Kingstanding and their overfilled china cabinet went with them.

Nanny Johnson had a sister Mabel who never married and she had haemophilia and apparently as a child, was 'highly strung'. When she was in her 40s she went to the local shop for some change for the gas meter, went home and put on her best nightie, combed her long hair and put her head in the gas oven. There had to be an inquest and the verdict was suicide by gas inhalation; it was a big shock for the family, it was in the local papers and the talk of the area. Nan also had a brother Harold and a brother Cyril, the 'babby', and she remained close to him all her life. He married a lady called Zillah and they lived in Alvechurch, Mom and Dad continued to visit Aunty Zillah until she died.

Mom's sister my Aunty Connie had several miscarriages before she gave birth to my cousin Diane in August 1949 on her own birthday and Lynn in 1952. They lived in Burbury Street opposite Nan and Grandpa Johnson. My cousins and I used to play together as children and my abiding memory of their house is the outside toilet. It had a wooden bench seat which had a crack in it so when you sat on it, it pinched your backside. A place to avoid if you could!

The cousins – Diane, Lynn, Stephen and me.

Aunty Connie used to work at home for someone from the Jewellery Quarter. The man used to deliver small wooden jewellery boxes which Aunty Connie then covered in material (sometimes fake snakeskin – very classy) and to do this she had to use glue. She always seemed to have a pot of glue, like a black cauldron on the stove and the smell of it used to pervade the house. My cousin, Diane still has the glue pot and it takes pride of place in her home with a plant in it.

Our extended family were very much part of our lives as we all lived so near to one another. You knew everything that was going on in the family and keeping any secrets was difficult. When the adults used to speak in whispers, we knew it was something they didn't want us to know but as the saying goes 'little pigs have big ears' so there was not much which escaped our attention.

Chapter 3

My Parents

Meeting

I t is a bit unclear how Mom and Dad met but they may have seen one another about as they lived fairly close, Mom in Burbury Street and Dad in Church Street. Or it may be that as both the Johnsons and the Hewitts liked to go to the pub and the children had to go into the pub garden, they may have met then. However they met, they started 'walking out' together when Mom was 17 and Dad 19, they got engaged when Mom was 19 and Dad 21. Mom was a bit of a romantic and, when she was young, she loved to read 'Pegs Paper', a women's magazine fuelling the fantasies of working class girls looking to marry a sheikh or rich man who they happened to bump into in Birmingham! A bit like Mills & Boon books. Mom designed her own engagement ring – a square shape filled with tiny diamonds – and Dad got one of his relatives who worked

at H Samuel in Hunters Road to get it made. They got engaged in this way... Dad took the ring round to Mom's house when it was ready, handed it to her and said "you may as well have this". Not perhaps the most romantic of proposals but they were married for 65 years so obviously it was a success.

Mom and Dad at home.

Mom and Dad's wedding, 1944.

Marriage

My mother got married on Easter Saturday 8 April 1944 to my father Ernest Eden Hewitt. They made a very handsome couple and when my dad grew a moustache, people used to say he looked like Clark Gable, the film star. As there was rationing, Mom got her wedding ring from a divorcee as well as her wedding veil. Dad's wedding ring had belonged to Uncle Charlie, Aunty Cis's husband who had died. Mom and Dad went to Evesham the next day for three days for their honeymoon on the bus. Mom looked smart in a pale blue dress with a black edge to edge coat and a small black hat and Dad read his cowboy book all the way on the bus much to Mom's annoyance. Aunty Connie and Uncle Ben rented a house opposite Nan and Grandpa's in Burbury Street and when Mom and Dad got married, they lived upstairs at this house; Dad converted the upstairs into a sort of flat for them. They had a two ring burner for a cooker and the first time Mom cooked boiled eggs, she cooked them separately in two saucepans because Dad liked his egg boiled longer!

When Mom married she gave up work at Lucas's as a comptometer operator. A comptometer was one of the first key driven mechanical calculators and she worked in the wages department. Mom said that after the war, married women were not supposed to work so some of them got married without telling their employer and wore their wedding rings on a chain around their neck. Once soldiers came back from the war, they were given their old jobs back where possible and so women had to relinquish their jobs.

Mom did not work again until later in life. She then worked as a supervisory assistant at a school in Aston until retirement age.

Family

Mom and Dad had a baby, Rex Harry, on 13 January 1947. Mom was in labour for three days and eventually went into hospital for the birth. She was always a bit vague why she chose the name Rex but as she and Dad loved films, it might have been from the film star, Rex Harrison. When Rex was born, it was one of the worst winters ever experienced in the UK and the snow stayed on the ground until March. The drifts were so deep outside the house that Dad had to cut an archway through the snow to get into the road. With no central heating, only a coal fire, when they used to try to make up Rex's feed in the kitchen, the warmth of the milk used to shatter the banana shaped glass bottles. They could not take Rex out in the pram until March. Tragically Rex died of leukaemia on 3 September the same year. No-one knew much about the disease in those days and it was pre-NHS. The whole episode was treated with little compassion and

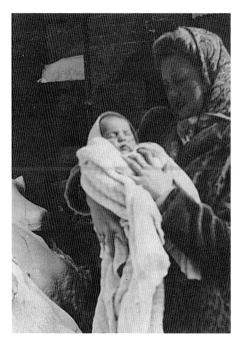 

Mom with Rex, 1947.   *Mom with Rex, in our garden 1947.*

there was no unrestricted visiting when your child was in hospital, you had to stick to visiting times. On 3 September 1947, Mom arrived at the hospital to visit Rex and was told he had died. The hospital had to carry out an autopsy because they were unsure of the cause of death. Rex had beautiful blond curls and when he was returned home for the funeral, all his curls had been shaved off and he was wearing a small linen cap to disguise the autopsy scar. Mom remembered that on the day of the funeral, Rex was in a tiny white coffin and the undertaker took the coffin out of the house, tucked under his arm. This was before the creation of the NHS in 1948, so there was no bereavement counselling then it was just a case of 'you'll have to get over it' but I don't think that Mom every really got over it. When Acorns Children's Hospice opened in 1988, Mom and Dad were supporters all their lives. For their Golden Wedding anniversary, they had a meal at the Botanical Gardens for family and neighbours. They requested no presents but donations for Acorns Hospice. If there had been such a service in place when Rex died, it would have made all the difference to be supported. After Rex's death, understandably Mom had deep depression. Eventually Connie and Ben began to invite Mom and Dad out on a Saturday to the motorcycle speedway at Perry Barr; they used to walk there and back. Mom suffered periods of depression throughout her life but they were

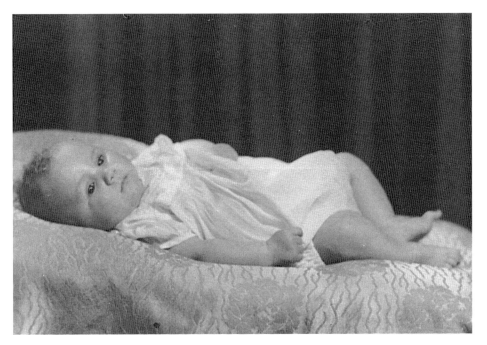

Studio portrait of Rex.

Card made for Rex's funeral.

not obvious to us as she did her best to hide them. They purchased a family grave for Rex in Handsworth cemetery but could not afford a headstone to put on it. She used to take me to the grave when I was very little, she used to walk three miles there and back; I used to call it 'the little garden'. One day whilst she was there, a thick mist came down over the cemetery which frightened her and she never went again although Dad still used to go. Just before she died, she was worried about Rex's grave and felt that she had neglected it. My parents had the deeds of the grave so my brother and I went to the cemetery to locate the plot, it was difficult to locate without a headstone but the staff found it for us. As it was a family grave, Mom's ashes were buried there and we had a headstone with Rex's details on 69 years after he died, Mom's details on and Dad said 'leave a gap for me at the bottom of the headstone' which we did. Dad's ashes are also now in the grave and the gap on the headstone filled.

I was born in the front room of 100 Church Street on 5 April 1949, I was delivered by a midwife. Dad went to fetch the midwife from up the street and wheeled her bike back to our house, carrying the gas and air cylinder which was

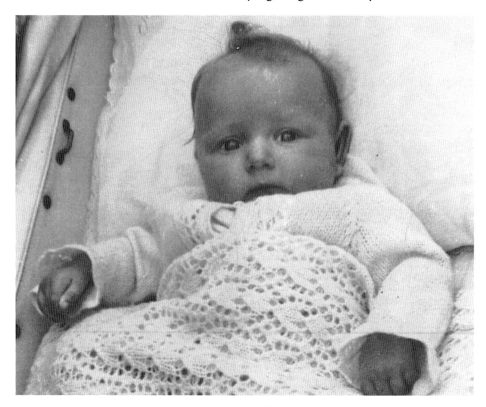

Me as a baby.

heavy. When the midwife went to use the cylinder, it was empty! The midwife asked my mom what I was to be called and Mom said she couldn't make up her mind between Gillian and Angela. The midwife said 'Angela Hewitt, stand up in class!' and then 'Gillian Hewitt, stand up in class! And decided that my name was to be Gillian. I felt short changed because I did not have a middle name.

My mom was very fashion conscious even though money was tight. Nanny Johnson used to enter her for beauty contests as a child and she often won. I have lots of photos of Mom at various stages in her life in various outfits and when I was little, she used to like to dress me well too.

Photo of Mom taken for a beauty contest.

Mom and me age 4 in our garden.

Me aged about 18 months.

She used to use Californian Poppy perfume, the only other choice at the time was 'Evening in Paris'. I used to sneak into her bedroom and dab myself with Californian Poppy out of the tiny bottle. I had a godmother, Aunty Frances, a friend of my mom's from Lucas days, and she was a good seamstress. I have a photo of myself age about three wearing a gingham dress with matching knickers; I had a gingham dress in every colour. I always wore black patent ankle strap shoes as a child and am still drawn to black patent shoes to this day. My favourite outfit Aunty Frances made me was a dress for one Christmas, it was red velvet with red sequins around the neck and I thought it was absolutely wonderful. She once let me choose my own material and I chose a pattern of bright orange big roses on a white background. It would probably have been better as curtain material but Aunty Frances dutifully made it into a dress for me.

Me in one of my gingham outfits.

Mom was always a blonde but as she got older, her hair started to fade a bit. She used to get Dad to bleach it for her prior to her going to the hairdressers. She used to sit on a dining chair in the living room while Dad applied the Hiltone hair colour and the smell of bleach was quite strong. She continued as a blonde until a few years before her death at the age of 87 but she always regretted having 'to let her hair go'.

Mom looking glamorous in 1941.

Dad left Gower Street School on Lozells Road at the age of 14. The building still stands and it was famous for having a playground on the roof – no Health and Safety problems in those days! I have his School Leaving Certificate dated 4 May 1934 which reads "A school prefect. Has held position of responsibility with great credit. Very energetic, reliable and trustworthy. Works well and aims at giving every satisfaction. Should do well". He certainly lived up to the remarks on his school certificate all his life. He left school on a Friday and started as an apprentice toolmaker at

Dad and his first car – a Morris Minor.

Lucas's in Chester Street, Aston on the following Monday. His first job was making the tea. He went to night school and got an OND in Engineering. The college wanted him to take his HND and the teacher came to Nanny Hewitt's to try to persuade him but he would not do it. He eventually became a toolmaker then tool room supervisor where he stayed until he retired at the age of 60. Being a toolmaker had its upside in terms of the gadgets he came up with but the downside was that he was a perfectionist when doing jobs at home. It took him ages to complete a job and he would often scrap what he had done and start all over again until he got it right, in his eyes.

My dad always cycled to work. I remember him leaving the house with his cycle clips on and when it was raining, he wore a yellow oilskin cape and sou'wester hat which certainly made him visible. He did not learn to drive until he was 46 and he was so nervous about his driving lessons on a Sunday morning, he could not eat his roast dinner, so his Sunday dinner was toast until he passed his test. He then bought a Morris Minor which expanded our travelling somewhat. He later progressed to the Austin Allegro and then later the Ford Fiesta. He was still driving his beloved 'R' reg Fiesta until two weeks before he died and said he felt safe, knowing that he had a car outside he could use whenever he wanted.

Mom and Dad went everywhere together; you would never see Molly without Ernie and vice versa as they got older. They enjoyed holidays in Britain and one of their favourite places was Torquay. Mom refused to fly anywhere but they ventured abroad on two occasions by coach to Austria. Dad had a cine camera so we have lots of films of their holidays. They were not drinkers; they used to say

Dad on a caravan holiday.

that they had seen too much of pubs when they were young and saw some of the effects alcohol had. Dad did not like beer or spirits and Mom and Dad might occasionally have a glass of wine if they went out for a meal but that was not a regular thing. At Christmas, they would buy Advocaat so that Mom could have a 'snowball' drink. This was a drink of advocaat, lemonade and lime juice but even this habit stopped eventually. They liked days out and if Dad could, he would usually manage to incorporate a visit to a steam railway in the itinerary. They visited relatives regularly until the older members of the family passed away.

Mom and Dad at a Lucas works do.

THE END

When Mom died, we wondered how Dad would cope as they had been together for so long and were never apart. But having looked after Mom while she was ill, Dad was very domesticated; his house was immaculate and he cooked good meals for himself, he enjoyed his food. He had daily newspapers, the Daily Express and the Birmingham Evening Mail and kept up to date with current events. He liked to discuss articles he had seen in the newspaper with us and was always interesting company. It never felt like we were talking to an old man as he was knowledgeable about what was going on in the world. He bemoaned the fact that engineering firms did not take apprentices as they used to as he felt that the manufacturing industry was the backbone of Britain. He still liked

Dad's 95th birthday treat.

to go out somewhere in the car, somewhere which usually involved steam railways. He started to build a model railway in the recess in the front room and was always tinkering with the layout, coming up with new ideas for it. He would go up into his workshop in the attic to make something for the railway and if there was a model railway fair locally, we would take him and he would always bring back something to put into his layout. He did not get around to actually finishing it so my brother now has it and will complete it.

For his 95th birthday, my brother, sister-in-law, my husband and myself took him for a cream tea on the Severn Valley Railway, one of his favourite haunts. One of my favourite photos is a reminder of this day, with Dad smiling and looking very smart in a new cream jacket and his usual cravat. He was ill for about two weeks before he died and one of the weeks, my brother and sister-in-law, I, my husband and my brother's eldest son, Paul, stayed at the house to look after him. This was a precious time for all of us as he was such a joy to look after. He died within a few days of going into hospital and my brother and myself were with him till the end.

Mom died after 65 years of marriage and Dad told us of a poem he had read in the Birmingham Evening Mail which he felt reflected the way he felt without Mom.

The poem is by a 19th century poet called Matthew Arnold and it is entitled 'Longing':

Come to me in my dreams, and then
By day I shall be well again!
For so the night will more than pay
The hopeless longing of the day.

Come, as thou cam'st a thousand times,
A messenger from radiant climes,
And smile on thy new world, and be
As kind to others as to me!

Or, as thou never cam'st in sooth,
Come now, and let me dream it truth,
And part my hair, and kiss my brow,
And say, My love why sufferest thou?

Come to me in my dreams, and then
By day I shall be well again!
For so the night will more than pay
The hopeless longing of the day.

Mom and Dad's Diamond Wedding Anniversary.

Chapter 4

World War II

Thanks to the world of television, films, the internet and other multimedia, we are probably quite well acquainted with the events of World War II but how did these events impact on Birmingham? Birmingham was a centre of industry and Lucas's, where my dad and Grandpa Johnson worked, made electrical equipment for military vehicles and were engaged by Rover to work on the Whittle jet engine project making the burners. Fisher and Ludlow made shell casings, bombs and Spitfire wings. The Aerodrome factory at Castle Bromwich made Spitfires and Lancaster bombers, Rover at Solihull made the Bristol Hercules engines and Austin at Longbridge made 500 military vehicles a week. Because of this, Birmingham was a prime target and was subject to heavy bombing; it was the third most bombed city after London and Liverpool with 1,852 tons of bombs being dropped. There were many casualties and one disaster remembered by Brummies is the bombing of the BSA (Birmingham Small Arms) factory. The factory made rifles and Sten guns and was bombed on 19 November 1940; 53 people were killed.

People's lives were devastated. They lost family members, homes and all their possessions in some cases. It is hard for us to imagine what it was like to live during these times but thanks to Mom and her recollections, I was given a glimpse of how the people of Lozells coped during these times. Although the times were so difficult, they were practical people, a 'make do and mend' generation who carried on in spite of the war because they were all in the same boat. As time went by and the war carried on, they took things in their stride and humour helped them to cope in circumstances we today would despair about. Rationing of food and clothes began in 1941 and did not end until 1949. The weekly food ration for an adult was:

4 oz bacon/ham
2 chops or similar
2 oz butter
2 oz cheese
4 oz margarine
4 oz cooking fat
3 pints milk
8 oz sugar
1lb preserves every two months
2oz tea
1 fresh egg (plus dried egg)
12oz sweets every four weeks

This was a small amount for an adult and people started to grow vegetables in their own garden and were very good at improvising meals out of very little. People kept chickens and rabbits to eat. Swapping ration coupons also went on, because Nan and Grandpa Hewitt both smoked, they would swap their sweet tokens with Mom and Dad for tobacco tokens. A lady who lived up the street had 11 children so she had milk tokens she would swap for other coupons. There was, of course, the 'black market' where goods such as the vital knicker elastic could be obtained 'under the counter' but all this was 'hush hush' and news about available goods was whispered from person to person.

When Mom was pregnant in 1947, she had to wait in a long queue at the greengrocers and she fainted. They took her round the back of the shop to recover and gave her a 'secret' banana, a rare prize in those days.

Clothing was rationed too, you received 66 tokens a year per adult but you couldn't get a lot out of that as the amount of tokens needed for each item was high:

11 coupons for a dress
2 coupons for nylons
8 coupons for men's shirts or trousers
5 coupons for women's shoes
7 coupons for men's shoes

8 coupons for underwear
16 coupons for a coat
13 coupons for a jacket

Again, people were very resourceful and parachutes were in great demand for underwear and even wedding dresses. Grey army blankets could be turned into coats or skirts. If a woman had no nylons, she could put gravy browning powder on her legs and draw a pencil line down for the seam. This worked as long as it didn't rain! Mom was always a bit of a 'clothes horse' and she managed to stay looking smart even during wartime by being creative with what little she had.

The war had a great impact on my parents and grandparents lives. Mom was 17 in 1939 and Dad 19 and the war continued all through their youth and start of their married life. My dad wanted to join the Marines but he was on reserved occupation at Lucas's during the war so this was not allowed. He joined the Home Guard and we did not know until we found the certificate amongst his papers, that he was a lance-corporal. He used to go to the gun battery at Perry Barr and his role was 'height finder'. This meant he had to calculate the height of the enemy airplanes and let the gunners know so that

Mom aged 21.   *Dad aged 19.*

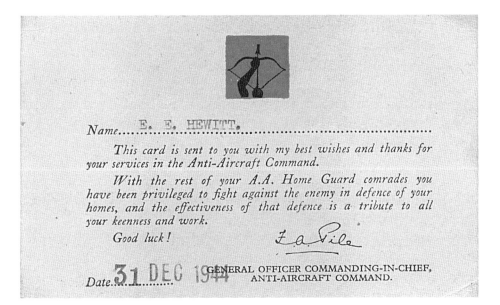

Name......E. E. HEWITT...

    This card is sent to you with my best wishes and thanks for your services in the Anti-Aircraft Command.

    With the rest of your A.A. Home Guard comrades you have been privileged to fight against the enemy in defence of your homes, and the effectiveness of that defence is a tribute to all your keenness and work.

    Good luck!

Date.**31 DEC 1944** GENERAL OFFICER COMMANDING-IN-CHIEF, ANTI-AIRCRAFT COMMAND.

Dad's thank you card from the Commander in Chief, Anti-Aircraft Command.

they could take correct aim and hopefully shoot them down with rockets launched by small batteries. Dad was good at Maths, a trait I did not inherit! When I struggled with Maths at school, Dad tried to help but got frustrated because I could not understand, it seemed so easy to him. Mom and Dad were courting at this stage, and Mom knitted Dad some socks and a balaclava to keep him warm when he was on Home Guard watch.

Courting during the war was a hazardous business and once when Dad was taking Mom home, there was an air raid over Burbury Street and they dashed into an entry to shelter. When Mom got home, she had chalk dust from the entry on the back of her coat and Grandpa Johnson went mad at her, thinking she had been 'up to no good'.

At the beginning of the war, they never went out without their gas masks but as the war continued, they got a bit lax about this. They all had to carry a National Identity Registration card with them and it had to be produced on demand so they dare not leave home without it. The identity card rule was not repealed until 1952, so I, little Gillian Hewitt born in 1949 had one, I still have my identity card.

Mom and Dad used to go to the Lozells picture house on a Tuesday evening. One Tuesday evening, they decided to go to the other picture house, the Villa Cross, instead. The Lozells cinema they usually went to was bombed that night resulting in fatalities. Everyone thought that Mom and Dad were there and when Nanny Johnson's neighbour came round to see Nan to offer her condolences and Mom opened the door to her, she thought she was seeing a ghost and fainted.

Another time, a UXB landed in Nursery Road and everyone had to be evacuated from the area. Mom was due to go for a job interview the next day and couldn't get into her house to get her clothes. She went to stay at Aunty Kitty's at number 76 Church Street and she lent her some clothes for the interview. The bomb disposal team were unable to diffuse the bomb and it went off, blowing all the windows out of the Johnson house and surrounding area.

Nanny and Grandpa Johnson's roof was hit by incendiary bombs and Mom remembered water cascading down the stairs into the living room while the fire men tried to dowse the flames.

My father was 21 in 1941 and he had presents for his birthday which he kept in a suitcase on top of his wardrobe. An incendiary came through the ceiling and onto the top of the wardrobe and he lost all his presents.

On another occasion, Nanny Hewitt was cooking pig's trotters in the scullery when another incendiary came through and she had to abandon the scullery. When she finally was able to return, the pig's trotters were no more – another black mark against Hitler! If she could, she would have added her pig's trotters to the War Reparations list.

Grandpa Hewitt had been in World War 1 and had been wounded at Ypres. I still have his pocket book from World War 1, including his will written in pencil leaving all his worldly goods, such as they were, to his wife. He is shown as having an honourable discharge due to a gunshot wound in his arm. During World War II, when the German bombers used to come over, he used to stand at the bottom of the entry, waving his fist at them and shouting 'Gertcha!' which is Brummie speak for 'Get away with you'. Nanny Hewitt used to like to go for a drink in the evening at the pub, the nearest being The Angel in Villa Street. She was sometimes turned back by the Fire Wardens if a raid was on and the area was unsafe. She simply used to find another way round to the pub.

Mom worked in the office at Lucas's, she worked on the first floor. She remembered standing at the office window watching a German plane come over, it was so low, she could see the pilot but it never occurred to her to move away from the window.

People tried to carry on as normal with their lives and if things were disrupted by war, they just found a way round them, like Nanny Hewitt going to the pub regardless. Hitler was not going to stop them, and the family were a great encouragement to one another. They pressed on, not giving in but carrying on with their family lives, and supporting one another in their sorrows and joys.

In the years when our Country

was in mortal danger

L/Cpl E E Hewitt

who served *from* 7/7/42 to 31/12/44

gave generously of his time and

powers to make himself ready

for her defence by force of arms

and with his life if need be.

George R.I.

THE HOME GUARD

Dad's Home Guard thank you certificate from the King.

Chapter 5

Our House

Mom and Dad lived at Aunty Connie's and Uncle Ben's in Burbury Street for a few years after they were married. They turned the upstairs into a tiny flat including a kitchen and they had to come downstairs to access the outside toilet. Then they heard by word of mouth that a house was becoming available for rent in Church Street so went round immediately to see if they could get it. Church Street was a long street bordered by Lozells Road at the top and then sloping downhill to Nursery Road at the bottom. The street was then divided into three with Wills Street and Graham Street crossing it. We lived towards the bottom of the middle section.

The house was built in late Victorian times and was very dark with all the walls painted dark brown and it took Dad ages with a blow lamp to remove the paint. They had little in the way of furniture and Mom made a kitchen cupboard out of an orange box (these were wooden boxes with a divider in the middle) turned on its side with a curtain to go across the front.

When they first moved in to number 100, the landlord lived next door, Mr Guck; he was in the jewellery trade. When Mrs Guck bought anything new in the way of clothing or bedding, she used to immediately hang it on the washing line in the garden outside before using it so that the neighbours could see she had something new. Mom used to say 'she's all kippers and curtains' this was a saying used about someone who had outward show eg. curtains but they were actually poor and could only afford to eat kippers.

One day Mr Guck told them that he was selling their house and his own next door. Mom and Dad could not get a mortgage to buy it but Grandpa Johnson's sister, Aunty Jinny (Jane) who had a sweet shop in Wellhead Lane

Perry Barr, lent them the £300 needed to buy it and they paid her back in monthly instalments.

100 Church Street was a terraced house which looked narrow from the outside but it went a long way back and so was deceptive. All the houses in the street were terraced and in between some of them was an entry. These were narrow passageways between the houses where you could gain access to the back gate. The entry was useful for sheltering from the rain if it started when we were playing out in the street. There was only room for one person to walk in an entry at a time and Mom's comment on people who were bow legged 'He couldn't stop a pig in an entry' gives you a visual idea of the width of the entry!

There was no front garden but there were two steep steps to the front door off the street. There was a long hall with first of all the front room off left, then some very steep stairs to the bedrooms, then the pantry leading down to a cellar then a living room and lastly a kitchen. There was no bathroom then, we didn't have one installed until I was age nine. Upstairs there were three bedrooms, one overlooking the front, one overlooking the back yard and one off a long gloomy landing which overlooked the garden. There was another flight of stairs from the landing outside the front bedroom; this led up to the attic. This had a fireplace in it so we wondered if at one time when the houses were first built in the late 19th century, they had a live-in maid. The attic was a great play area for my brother and myself, we could play houses as there were bits of old furniture up there. When my brother was older, he and Dad built a model railway and my brother made little figures for the layout, including a bride and groom outside the church with a photographer and camera. My brother inherited my dad's tool making skills and is still a stickler for perfection whenever he attempts any DIY. In later years, after we had left home, Dad used the attic as his workshop and had a tool bench and all sorts of tools and all the bits of plastic and wood he kept – 'you never know when they will come in useful!' If ever we wanted anything repairing, he could always find something up in the attic which would do the trick.

We had a yard outside the back door which went up past the old outside toilet and dustbin store. Past the yard, there was a long area of grass. The end of the garden faced the end of the gardens in Anglesey Street. To the right of the garden was a wall where the ground dropped away the other side. Below this wall was a commercial garage which eventually fell into disrepair. The access to this garage was in Graham Street; it was eventually demolished and the land became part of next door's garden. As we got older, we didn't play much in the garden, the streets were our playground.

Me aged 2 and Mom in our garden.

My abiding memory of the house was mice!! Being an old property, it was a 'des res' for mice and I was frightened of them, still am! We would be watching the TV in the corner of the living room when a mouse would whizz past in front of us and disappear into the skirting board, or wainscoting as we called it. I was once going up the stairs and a mouse came lolloping past me the other way, they got in everywhere. One time Mom made a trifle and put it on top of the fridge in the pantry to keep cool, a mouse was running along the shelf above it and jumped off, straight into the trifle. Dad fought a losing battle with mice but I think he sort of won in the end as I don't remember seeing so many of them or maybe I just got used to sharing a house with them.

There was a routine to housework, Mondays was always washday when you had Sunday's leftovers for dinner, Tuesday was bedrooms and so on through the week. This was fitted around daily food shopping. Mom had a vacuum cleaner in the 50s, it was a Hoover cylinder type, it was made of grey metal and looked like a bomb; it was very heavy. She kept this for years and when she eventually retired it in favour of a more lightweight model, Dad took it up to his workshop in the attic and kept it for years. Its powerful suction was great for getting up sawdust. There were summer curtains to be changed and washed and replaced with winter curtains. Neighbours took it in turns to swill the entry with water and the front steps kept clean in case anybody called.

Outside, beyond the kitchen, there was a dustbin cubby hole and the outside toilet. I remember in the winter, Dad used to lag the pipes with old rags and put a paraffin heater in there as it was so cold and the pipes might freeze. During the night, we used a potty or 'po' under the bed which Mom emptied every morning. When they had the bathroom built, the dustbin shed and toilet were demolished and the bathroom was built next to the kitchen with a lobby in between the kitchen and the bathroom. Up to that point, we had been washed in the kitchen sink and once a week the big tin bath was lugged in from outside and we had a bath in the kitchen. Mom used to light the oven and leave the door open so that we had some heat and she filled the bath from the little boiler she had for washing clothes. To go from this to a real bathroom was luxury!

Dad was a top class DIY man. He only renovated one room at a time, depending on finances, so some rooms such as the front room were not updated until I was growing up. I can remember Dad doing DIY jobs while my brother and I played around him, hiding under the doors he was sanding.

He once varnished the doors in the sitting room and used one of Mom's hair combs to make a pattern on the doors. It would probably not pass muster today in a 'Changing Rooms' programme, but it was quite innovative at the time. As my parents got a bit more financially better off, they used to have a decorator come in to wallpaper the rooms, his name was Jack Barber and he had a shop on Nursery Road. We used to look at the wallpaper sample books with Mom to see which we liked but there was not the variety there is now and we usually ended up with something beige!

Dad was the ultimate gadget man – if there was something he could make to make life easier, he would invent it and make it, even when he was in his 90s. The classic piece was the cup turntable. Mom observed that they always seemed to be using the same cups as they were put at the front of the cupboard after washing up. He therefore made a cup turntable out of wood, a circular piece of wood with holes in for cups. When the cups were washed up these were put in the holes and then the turntable turned round to make sure that the next set of cups were used. It was one of those things you would not think you needed but was useful once you had it. My brother still has this marvellous invention.

Of course, in my childhood, we did not have central heating, in fact Mom and Dad did not have it installed until later in life so there are many memories of being cold in the house. In winter there used to be ice on the inside of the bedroom window as well as the outside and it took courage to get out of bed and put your feet on the ice cold lino, carpets were a thing of the future. There was a fireplace in my bedroom but it only had a fire lit in it when I was ill. An open fire sounds better than it actually is. When you sat by it, the front of your body was warm but your back was freezing, if you sat by the fire too long, the front of your legs got burnt. Nan used to say that she could always pick out a lazy woman – their legs were mottled at the front from sitting in front of the fire instead of doing their chores! The fire in the living room was the main source of heat and I remember Christmases where Stephen and I stood shivering while Dad tried to get the fire going so we could open our Christmas presents. He used to put strips of wood in the grate, tie folded newspaper into a knot and put them on with the coal and if the fire would not get going, he would use either a metal draw plate of a piece of newspaper which inevitably went up in smoke! Who can forget the metal toasting fork which you held in front of the open fire to make your toast, ours had an extending handle and if you weren't careful, the bread would drop off the end into the ashes. You just scraped the ashes off and carried on. We had a cellar which was accessed by stairs down from the pantry. The cellar had an arched recess on one wall and we thought it was either for wine (delusions of grandeur!) or for cold storage of food. We used to store coal in the cellar and the coal man used to deliver the coal in sacks and pour it through a grating outside in the street into the cellar, it made a loud rumbling noise as it fell. Dad then used to go down with a shovel and a bucket to bring up some of it to keep by the fire. One day he came up from the cellar with a frog on the shovel, I don't know how that got in with the coal! I remember it was a big event when we had the chimney sweep come to clean the chimney, all the furniture was covered in dust sheets and we used to go outside to see if we could see the brush come out of the top of the chimney. If you did not get the chimney cleaned regularly, you used to get a fall of soot from the chimney which managed to cover everything in the room with black dust.

When we had a cold or similar, Mom used to warm camphorated oil in front of the fire and rub it on our chests under our vests, our vests and pyjamas were warmed on the fireguard. When Mom was young, she was made to wear a liberty bodice, a sort of vest like garment with buttons which you wore over your vest. These came about in the 1920s when women abandoned corsets for something a little less constricting and Mom hated these when she was young so no daughter of hers was going to wear one as other children of my age did.

The first neighbours I remembered were Mr and Mrs Wilson who we shared the entry with. Mrs Wilson was from Derbyshire and regularly wore an overall. They had two daughters, Joyce and then quite a bit later on, June who was a bit older than me. When Joyce got married, she and her husband lived with Mr and Mrs Wilson until they got their own house, Mr Wilson converted the pantry into a kitchen for them; it must have been a tight squeeze because the pantry was tiny. Later on, Mr Wilson had a heart attack and Dad used to get him books to read from the library. When Mr and Mrs Wilson left, it was bought by an Irishwoman, Mrs McCauley, a widow who always wore black, who moved in with her daughters. They took in lodgers so there was always something going on in the house. Her youngest daughter Chrissie married one of the lodgers, Johnny Docherty. We went to her wedding and after the reception, they came home and Chrissie could be seen cooking the tea in the kitchen still wearing her wedding dress. They stayed in Church Street for many years.

Mom and Dad never moved from this house and it went through many transformations over the years. although the original coving and ceiling light plaster in the living room were kept. Mom died in the house at the age of 87 after being looked after by Dad for about 18 months. Dad carried on living there, still going up into his workshop to 'pither about' as Mom used to call it or making a model railway in the recess of the front room. He died in 2016 at the age of 96, the longest living resident of the Hewitt family; I used to call him 'the king of Church Street'.

Dad cooking in his kitchen.

Mom with Rex in Handsworth Park.

My christening, Aunty Frances (holding me) was my godmother.

Me, holding my brother like a sack of potatoes in our garden.

The four of us with Grandpa Hewitt.

Mom, me and Stephen ready for Aunty Hilda's wedding.

Mom and Dad's Silver Wedding Anniversary.

Mom, me and Stephen in our garden.

Mom, Dad and me aged 3 at Paignton.

Dad on holiday.

Chapter 6

Our Family
and Home Life

I have already described the tragedy of Rex's birth and death and my own entrance into the world. My brother was born in the front room on 4 May 1953 when I was four. My mother had been asking my father for weeks to take the mattress downstairs to the front room in time for the birth but he hadn't got round to it. When she suddenly went into labour, she went downstairs and he rolled the mattress down after her! He went to get his mother and the midwife and when the midwife came in the front door, she was calling 'Hold on' to my mother but it was too late. My brother was born very quickly, in about 30 minutes, and as he was a big baby, over 9lbs, it caused my mom a few problems. People locally used to say he looked 'as big as a Bootle's baby'. I never understood what this meant until recently. Apparently 'Bootles'

Studio photo of me with my brother.

Baby' was a book written by John Strange and subtitled 'A Story of the Scarlet Lancers'. The synopsis is that a captain's secret wife plants a baby on a friend who weds her when the captain is killed. I presume that this Bootles' Baby must have been rather large! As children, we were often called by strange names, if we were dawdling, Mom used to say 'Come on, Fanny Fanakapan'. This was the name of a character in a song by Gracie Fields but was used in everyday language. She also called me 'Emma Boot', I have no idea why and my Aunty Connie used to call me Nana from Gilliana Banana. As the saying goes, 'you can call me what you like as long as you call me for my tea'.

I have vague recollections of earlier months when Mom was in bed being sick and my nan with a soda water syphon in her hand as she was making Mom drink soda water, which she hated, I presume this was morning sickness. I also remember my father asking me what I would like for a present and I said 'a bike', this wasn't the answer he wanted to hear because the present I was going to get was a baby brother or sister. I was taken into the front room by my nan to see the baby after his birth and Mom asked me what I wanted to call him, I said 'Jack' because my name was Gill but this did not go down too well. He was called Stephen and my dad went to register his name, Mom sent him back to the Register Office because she wanted him to have 'Ernest' as a middle name. Mom used to keep Nurse Harvey's Gripe Water in a cupboard in the kitchen when Stephen was a baby, I used to love the taste of it and would sneak a quick swig when no-one was looking. I don't think it is used nowadays because in those days it contained alcohol. No wonder I used to like sucking the cork in the bottle!

When we were very young, Mom used to take us down the 'welfare', the Carnegie welfare centre in Hunters Road. She used to get the National Dried Milk from there and the empty tins were useful for all sorts of things eg keeping maggots in, collecting blackberries and storage for screws. We used to have orange juice with cod liver oil as well, I hated it as well as the spoonfuls of malt Mom used to give us in the winter to 'build us up'.

Shopping

When I was little, Mom used to shop for food every day as fridges were not around until I was about 10. We usually went shopping with Nanny Johnson as well and there were three shopping areas we visited. One was the Lozells Road where there was a Baines cake shop (their bakery was in Finch Road) and I loved their doughnuts with confectioner's cream in and also their ginger cakes with icing on the top. There was a Woolworths and a Marsh and Baxter's butchers where we used to buy pork dripping to have on toast (I did not like the jelly on the top) and everyone seemed to know everyone else.

My parents actually bought a fridge in 1959 and I recorded this event in my school diary. We couldn't go on holiday that year because the fridge cost £60 (the equivalent today would be about £1,140). For laundry, after starting out with a tub and a podger (or maid), Mom progressed to a small electric boiler, this was used for laundry and filling the tin bath. She later progressed to a Hotpoint Countess automatic washing machine with a mangle which few people in the street had.

We sometimes went up the Villa Road leading to Handsworth and the main shop I remember there was Wilkinson's. It was a large hardware store selling household goods where the floor manager at the door dressed in a smart suit, when we went in my mom and nan used to say 'Good Morning, Mr Durham' and he used to reply 'Good Morning, ladies'. I have learned since that this shop was owned by the brother of the Wilkinson who founded Wilkinson stores, the famous Wilko of today.

Every Friday we went down to 'the flat' which was a row of shops in Hockley. We used to go into the butchers for our meat and the butcher was called Arthur, he had a red face, a serious comb-over and very red hands and was exceedingly polite. Mom treated us to the delights of sheep's brains on toast – yuk! Tripe – even more yuk! And sheep's heart which, once it was carved up, left us with very little to eat. I didn't like meat much as a child, the taste or the texture, and I have been a vegetarian for many years.

If we were very good, we could go to Norton's department store up Key Hill. This was an old fashioned department store which sold haberdashery, clothes etc and had one of those antiquated tube systems for sending money round the shop. But their crowning glory was the restaurant which was on the top floor, we were allowed to have orange juice and sit on the stools by the window overlooking Hockley. This did not happen very often as Norton's prices were a bit out of our league. We very rarely went into Birmingham but if we did it was 'going into town' although Birmingham is a city not a town.

There were the local shops too. There was a corner shop on the corner of Church Street and Graham Street, this was run by a couple called the Wallaces and they sold general grocery items but more importantly to us, they sold bottles of pop. Very occasionally we were allowed to fetch some pop from Wallaces, my favourite was Tizer which used to leave orange marks round your mouth. My least favourite was ice cream soda but to have pop at all was a rare treat.

There was a traditional grocery shop on the corner of Burbury Street and Wills Street, it had a wooden floor and gold lettering on the door and windows. It used to smell of bacon and coffee, the bacon was sliced on a bacon slicer on the counter and the cheese was cut with a cheese wire. It seemed to me to be a 'posh' shop but they always had a cat in the window sitting among the food so it probably wasn't that high class.

On the corner of Church Street and Nursery Road was a hardware shop which I think was called Badnadges although we called it Bandages. This was crammed with all sorts of DIY and hardware goods and smelt of paraffin, Dad used to send me down to get his screws when he was doing yet another DIY job. Whenever we went to the local shops, Mom would stop for a chat with the locals, there were certain phrases which used to crop up regularly in these conversations. If you looked sad, you had a 'face as long as Livery Street', if the baby was crying, people would say 'Give the babby a piece'. A piece is what Brummies call a slice of bread and butter or marge. If they heard a story which they thought was incredible, they used to say 'never in the reign of pigs pudding'. If there was a woman of a dubious character, they used to say she was from 'the back of Rackhams', this was a big department store in Birmingham and the rumour was that behind this store was a red light district.

If as children we seemed to be trying too hard to do something, Mom used to say 'Don't force it Phoebe!' If anyone was in pain they used to say 'It's agony Ivy'. Someone who had bulging eyes was said to have eyes that 'stood out like chapel 'at pegs' and, of course, your hands were your 'donnies' as in 'you've got dirty donnies'. If a woman in the area was being snobbish or getting ideas above her station, it was a case of 'Who does she think she is? Lady Muck?' And I remember one great disappointment early in life when Dad said he was going 'to see a man about a dog', I was expecting him to return with a puppy!

Once when I was very young, the man next door to us died and his widow asked if Mom and some of the neighbours would organise the tea and sandwiches for after the funeral which people did in those days. Mom had to take me with her and the deceased lay in an open coffin on the front room table. I remember running past the door to the front room as I was frightened of the coffin. Everyone in the street used to shut their curtains on the day of a funeral.

A few houses down from Nanny Johnsons in Burbury Street, there was the 'outdoor' (off licence) and even as a young child they used to let me collect a jug of beer to take to Nan. Next to it was a cobblers shop, I never knew the cobbler's name but called him 'Mr Right Ho Yes' because that's what he said whenever you took shoes to him to be repaired. I never heard him say anything else. He was very good at his job and your shoes looked a great deal better when you collected them than when you took them in.

We eventually had a TV when I was about five and I remember one Saturday afternoon, when Grandpa Johnson and Uncle Ben came round to watch the FA cup final with Dad. Mom took me to the pictures to see, 'The King and I' which I thought was lovely and romantic and I felt very grown up going to the pictures with my mom. Every Sunday evening Nan and Grandpa Johnson used to call at our house on their way to the 'Waterloo', they used to stay a while to watch the TV but would then go on to see their friends in the pub. Although we had a TV, we still listened to the radio. There was 'Workers' Playtime', The Archers, Listen with Mother and one of our favourite programmes, Two Way Family Favourites. The presenter on this was Cliff Michelmore and he used to read out requests for music from the armed forces amongst others, the other presenter was stationed somewhere else and reported back to Cliff. One of the presenters was Judith Chalmers and Cliff Michelmore used to ask her in his cultured voice 'What's the weather like where you are Judith?' For some unaccountable reason we used to think this very amusing and we used it as a catchphrase in our family, even mimicking the posh voice.

We had our main meal – dinner – at lunch time and sandwiches for tea. I used to like sugar butties, bread and margarine liberally sprinkled with granulated sugar, it's a wonder I still have my own teeth. We also had banana sandwiches and on Sunday, bread and butter which we had to eat before we could have any tinned fruit. I liked tinned fruit but did not like the fluted fruit spoons, they were so old, the covering had worn off and they were rough on your mouth.

I was a 'fussy' eater apparently and when I was about three, if Mom asked what I wanted to eat, I always said 'boyd' (boiled) ham. This went on for about six weeks until I got bored with it. Once when I was little and went on holiday with my parents to a boarding house, the woman who owned the house was almost in despair because I did not want to eat anything. She tried everything including making pink blancmange to tempt me and Mom was embarrassed because of the trouble the landlady was going to which I ignored. My mom said I was a 'wilful' child but I prefer my brother's version, I was not wilful, but 'spirited'.

I don't remember fruit featuring much in our household as a child but as I was born in 1949, there was still rationing. However when I was older, Mom bought some apples which we tucked into. This led to her famous remark 'I am not buying any more apples, you only eat them'! On Friday nights, Dad would bring a sweet treat from Woolworths; my favourite was Caramac, a caramel bar made by Mackintosh, hence the name Caramac.

My recollection of childhood is like a kaleidoscope, I can see the events in my mind but they are not in any order. I remember being in a school hall on Coronation Day in 1953 and receiving a skipping rope with red, white and blue wooden handles. I remember queuing with Aunty Hilda on the stairs at Lewis's when she was taking me to see Father Christmas and Uncle Holly. She took me to a circus and we sat in the front row, I was frightened by the clowns and to be honest, still try to keep my distance. I must have been about three when Mom and Dad took me on holiday on a train to Paignton, Dad had got hold of this wonderful invention called a collapsible plastic cup so that I could have a drink on the train. The design was not a good one and Dad had to put his handkerchief round the cup to stop all the drink from escaping. Dad, Uncle Ben and Grandpa Johnson used to go to swim at the brine baths in Droitwich on Sunday mornings and Dad used to bring back a small bottle of pineapple juice for Mom.

Dad used to take my brother trainspotting as he had done as a boy, I used to go occasionally and read the engine numbers out to Stephen so that he could mark them off in his Ian Allan trainspotting book.

On Saturday afternoons, Dad had the same routine; he had polony sandwiches for his tea (it sounded very exotic to me!) and then checked his football pools. Occasionally he would let me fill in his football coupon but never won anything.

On Sunday mornings, we used to go down to Nanny and Grandpa Hewitts with my dad and he used to vacuum the house for them. He also used to give them some money which did not please Mom too much as she thought they spent it on their cigarettes and whisky. But Dad was a dutiful son and continued with the weekly donations until they died.

One day, I must have been about eight, Mom and Dad took us to Handsworth on the bus and we walked up and down several roads looking at houses. I think that it was in their minds to move to Handsworth but in the end, for whatever reason, they decided against it and we remained in Lozells. A Handsworth address was something to be proud of, if you lived in Handsworth Wood, you were only one step down from royalty! And as for Sutton Coldfield – that was for royalty!

As Dad worked for Lucas's, we always went to the famous Lucas Christmas parties in Great King Street. There were loads of children at these parties and the lady workers used to look after us, we called them 'Aunty'. There was entertainment, food and a present – what more could we ask for!

There was great consternation in our family when Dad came home from work and announced that he had been asked if he would go to Madras in India to help set up a toolroom for Lucas's. All the family could go too. This was unheard of and there was much deliberation about what to do with important questions being asked such as 'Can we take Cornflakes to India?' In the end Mom and Dad didn't go because of our education. If we had gone, we would have returned to the UK the year before I was due to take GCE O-levels and not having an English education might prejudice my chances. Also my brother would have had to go to a boarding school thousands of miles from Madras and Mom would not allow that. It would have been a big step for a family who had never been outside Britain and were not by nature adventurous.

We used to see 'Watch With Mother' on TV, Bill and Ben the flowerpot men, Andy Pandy and the Woodentops. My earliest memory is of watching Muffin the Mule performing on the piano, my mom told me that the lady with Muffin the Mule was Annette Mills. I loved 'The Lone Ranger' and 'Champion the Wonder Horse'. My parents liked to watch 'What's My Line' with Eamonn Andrews as compere, 'Perry Mason' with Raymond Burr in the starring role and a variety show called 'Sunday Night at the London Palladium'.

I went to Brownies at the Villa Street Methodist church at Villa Cross, I was not a 'sixer' but a 'seconder' in the Fairies. We learnt various skills, such as how to clean shoes properly (remember to polish the bit underneath between the sole and heel!) and sewing. I did not go on to join the Guides because when I had passed the 11 plus, I thought that I would not have time for anything else but school.

Sunday school and church

I was four when my brother was christened at St Silas church and as we were coming out of the church after the service, I saw a lot of children coming out of the door of the schoolroom on the other side of the yard and I asked what they were doing. I was told that they had come from the Sunday School and I told Mom and Dad that I wanted to go to Sunday School. So I joined at the age of four and attended regularly, my parents used to take me up the road and then eventually I used to go on my own. We used to have Sunday School anniversaries once a year when I had a new dress and white lace gloves to complete the ensemble, we also used to receive prizes of books for Sunday School attendance and I still have two of mine. There was a Mission Hall belonging to the church which was on the corner of Nursery Road. On the Monday evening after the anniversary, we used to repeat the performance so all that effort in learning the songs was not wasted. The Sunday School Christmas parties were also held in the Mission Hall and my abiding memory of the food was fish paste sandwiches, doughnuts and weak orange squash, a rather strange combination but we weren't too concerned because there were games afterwards. We used to have Sunday School outings, mainly to the Lickey Hills as you could get there on the bus. Although my parents did not go to church, I was confirmed in church at age 17 and have continued in the Christian life to this day. It has been a rich part of my life and continues to be so.

Chapter 7

Holidays and Days Out

Dad and Mom always took us on holiday for a week during the industrial fortnight, the end of July beginning of August. Dad used to save in a Lucas savings club so that we could have a holiday. We used to go by coach as Dad did not have a car. There was no pre-booking of coaches then so to get to where we wanted to go, we used to arrive at Digbeth coach station on the Saturday and wait until the coaches came in. There was then a mad dash to get on a coach and as it was the 'industrial fortnight', there were lots of people trying to do the same thing. Sometimes we would get on a coach and have to get off because there were not enough seats for the four of us. You could also guarantee that Dad would want to go to the Gents just as we were due to leave so, even as a child, I found the whole thing very stressful. On the coach, we always had the same sweets, I liked sherbet lemons, and I used to eat them like they were going out of fashion and get a sore

Me and Stephen on holiday.

Me and Stephen on holiday.

Me with that rubber ring in the sea.

tongue! Stephen liked barley sugars. We went to Weymouth, Cliftonville, Aberystwyth but our favourite place was the Isle of Wight. One year we went for two weeks and the weather was so hot, the sand on Sandown beach was too hot to walk on! On beach holidays, Dad used to build us a sand 'motor boat' to sit in, it was in perfect proportion of course and certainly an improvement on the usual sand castles.

One year, Mom and Dad bought me a red and white rubber ring to play with in the sea. I loved it and started trying to swim in it. I got carried away and when I looked up, the pier was quite a way behind me! I didn't know how to get back but fortunately a

Stephen in the sea.

couple in a small boat saw me and rescued me. We used to joke that Mom and Dad tried hard to get rid of me by sending me out to sea in a rubber ring. They also lost my brother after he wandered off when he was little on the beach at Cliftonville. It was panic stations looking for a blond haired little boy wearing red trunks, there were so many of them on the beach! Fortunately they found him. My parents weren't particularly careless, the beaches in those days were so packed, you needed eyes in the back of your head.

We used to stop in boarding houses and when we were very small, my mom's mom and dad used to come with us. As we got older, this stopped and Mom felt very uncomfortable when she had to tell my nan and grandpa that we were going on holiday on our own. I think they were OK about it and they did go on holidays by themselves. My granddad's concession to going on holiday was to take one spare collar for his shirt as he always wore a suit on

Nan and Grandpa Johnson on holiday in later years.

holiday. The year we went to Cliftonville, Dad fell down some steps onto the beach and Mom and he went to the hospital as he thought he had broken his toe. They put us into the care of Nan and Grandpa. When Mom and Dad got back later, we were being minded by the landlady of the boarding house as my nan and grandpa had gone to the pub at their usual time! Childcare then is not what it is now! I only remember once been looked after by my Nanny Johnson when Mom had to go somewhere and I must have been young because Stephen had not been born. When she got back my mom asked if I had been alright, Nan said I had but when Nan ate the tube of Smarties Mom had left for me, I had cried but she didn't know why!

During some of the holidays, Dad used to buy railway 'runabout' tickets for the second week of the holiday. This gave us unlimited travel around the Midlands to various places such as Coventry, Lichfield, Rugby and Worcester. We used to go to Snow Hill station on the bus, and spend all day 'train hopping'. Our special treat on these journeys was 'railway cake'. This was a small slab of fruit cake wrapped in cellophane which you bought at the refreshment room. In our family, it is still called 'railway cake' to this day.

Mom and Dad usually took us out on Saturdays when the weather was good and we went on the bus to places such as Solihull Park, St Nicholas Park, Warwick and of course, the Lickeys. We used to like to go blackberry picking at the Lickeys and collected them in an old National Dried Milk tin – you could get quite a lot in one of those. Dad would take us to Knowle on the train and we would walk across fields to Dorridge and then take another train back home. He would also take us for a walk along the canal at Lapworth and as a rare treat, we would stop off at the Navigation pub and sit in the garden. We would all have a lemonade and Stephen and I would have some Smiths crisps with the little blue packet of salt in the bag.

Within walking distance of our house was Handsworth Park. It was

Dad, me and Stephen at Solihull park.

created during Victorian times and had a boating lake and it was a favourite for recreational walks. Mom and Aunty Connie used to take me and my cousin Diane there in our prams to get some fresh air and when we got older, there was a playground with a 'witches hat' to climb on.

When I was little we also used to go to the Botanical Gardens in Edgbaston, although I called it the 'Bonatical Gardens'. I was fascinated by the tropical house and fish ponds.

We were fortunate because Mom and Dad used to take us out regularly on the bus or train and we discovered many interesting places in the West Midlands which broadened our horizons and interests.

Me on holiday.

Chapter 8

Toys and Playtime

We did not play much in the garden, when we got to school age we often played outside on the street with the children who lived close by. Anyone from outside our little patch was told to 'Go and play up your own end!' We played hopscotch, chalking out the squares on the pavement and using a little piece of slate to throw onto the squares. We played tag and if you got back to base before the person who was 'on', you called out 'Ackee 123'. I don't know where this phrase came from, my husband said that when they played it as children, they used to say 'leaky 123'. We also played hide and seek (this was where the entrys came in useful), and a game we called 'hitting Arthur Place'. It sounds violent but there was a plaque on the wall over our entry with the name on it 'Arthur Place', level with the front bedroom window. We used to throw a tennis ball at the Arthur Place plaque to see how many times we could hit it without breaking a window which seemed exciting at the time.

Much to my regret, I was not allowed a bike, but I did get to ride a trike on one of our holidays. I did have a scooter when I was about seven, it was a Triang scooter in red and yellow and I used to love going round the streets on it. One evening, I was out on my scooter and I just kept going on it and ended up at Aston in what is now Newtown Row. I only realised how far I had gone as I was whizzing past 'The House That Jack Built', a furniture shop in Aston. Oblivious to time, when I got back Mom and Dad were up in arms thinking I had been abducted or had an accident. I did have a secondhand metal swing and was told not to get on it wearing my best dress as it could get oil from the swing on it. Of course I did just that!

On holiday riding a trike.

On my swing.

My godmother was Aunty Frances, a friend of Mom's from work. She did not marry until her 40s so was a regular visitor at our house. She bought me a hula hoop when they became popular. I practised swirling it in the living room and knocked the goldfish bowl off the top of the TV with it so I was banned to the yard with it.

One year for Christmas, Dad made me a doll's house out of wood and it was lovely. There was a central door and rooms either side of the door and the stairs were covered in brown velvet by Mom to look like carpet. One year he made my brother a fort out of wood, it was painted grey with black lines to look like bricks and even had crenellations on the top. These must have taken him ages and I wish we had taken a photo of them or kept them.

Dad built a go-kart for Stephen, it was made out of wood with pram wheels and because Dad had designed and produced it, it had the most advanced braking system in the street!

We had a sideboard at the back of the living room, with two opening doors and when my brother was small, he used to empty out the cupboards and sit in the sideboard and this was his 'car'.

As a child, I was not a big fan of dolls and once marched up the yard and put them all in the dustbin. I did keep one doll and when I was asked the

Me with a doll in our garden.

My doll 'Pat Pending'.

My teddy today.

name of the doll, I said it was 'Pat Pending' as this was the name stamped on the back of the doll. I was grown up before I realised that this stood for 'Patent Pending' but I still have her and she will always be Pat Pending to me. I still have my original teddy bear given to me by my Aunty Kitty when I was one year old, it is very threadbare but I couldn't part with it.

My brother had Meccano sets and toy trains and I once had a chemistry set, I was intrigued by the test tubes and the copper sulphate crystals which turned the water blue. I usually had an encyclopaedia for Christmas and was fascinated by the illustrations in it.

We did not get to keep many of our toys once we had finished with them. Mom was a great 'thrower out' so they disappeared, never to be seen again.

On Saturday mornings, I used to go to the Villa Cross picture house to see the children's films, I used to go with Margaret who lived next door to us and was a bit older than me. I watched one film, 'Dan Dare and the Martians', and it really frightened me, I was unable to sleep that night in case the Martians came for me!

We had a lot of freedom in our childhood and would spend all day outdoors, only coming in for something to eat. Our world felt safe and we were shielded from the unpleasant things of life and we kept our innocence longer. The adult world was of little interest to us as long we could play with our friends.

Chapter 9

Primary and Junior School Life

Our local Junior and Infants school was Anglesey Street School, known as the 'Ango'. It was a red brick building just round the corner from where we lived so the children from the middle and bottom section went there. If you lived in the top half of Church Street, you would go to St Silas School.

I learned to read at an early age, Dad used to read to me regularly until he realised I was reading for myself so by the time I went to school I was a good reader. I remember one story book in particular that Dad used to read, and I can still see the illustrations in my mind's eye. It was about Father Christmas on his travels through a wood in the snow but he didn't know he had a hole in his sack and all the toys were dropping out. This book always made me feel sad as it was very real to me and I thought that the children would have no toys for Christmas. As I got older, I had a set of classic books in red covers which were from Woolworths – I remember reading Treasure Island, Little Women, Good Wives, Jo's Boys, Heidi and Robinson Crusoe to name just a few. At the age of eight, Mrs Ainger, my teacher asked me to do a reading test at school and I remember that one of the words I pronounced correctly was 'belligerent' (probably because I had been told I was a few times!), it transpired that I had a reading age of 13.

My Dad was a reader; he used to read cowboy books and then books by Alistair MacLean, Desmond Bagley and other adventure writers, whereas my

School hall.

mother did not read a lot. However, when she was very ill at the end of her life, she wanted to read a book published in 1862 called 'Mrs Halliburton's Troubles' by Mrs Henry Wood; this was a good old Victorian melodrama. It stuck in her mind because this was the book my nan had read on her honeymoon. We managed to get hold of a copy via the internet and Dad read it to Mom. They spent an enjoyable(?) few months reading it all the way through; it must have been a labour of love!

My first foray into school life was not a happy one. My brother was born when I was four and I started school soon after and resented the fact that he was at home while I had to go to school! The school was just round the corner from us in Anglesey Street and every morning, Mom had to carry me to school crying and protesting all the way. The staff said to her that if she came back in about half an hour and looked through the classroom door, she would see that I was as right as rain. Which I was! In the first class, I was a milk monitor and also played the part of the angel in the nativity, draped in a white sheet with a cardboard halo. In the winter, I used to wear a hand knitted bonnet and mittens attached through my coat sleeves by a string so they did not get lost.

There was also the school tuck shop during the morning break! Jammy Dodgers and Wagon Wheels which were almost the size of wagon wheels were sold from a desk in the corridor.

On the school photograph taken when I was about seven or eight, there are 38 of us in the class which was normal for those days.

Mr Powell was the school caretaker who lived in a red brick house on the school site, he wore a blue boiler suit and when you saw him, he was usually carrying a bucket with sawdust in it to put over 'accidents'.

Both Stephen and I caught nits from school and Mom's method of dealing with them was to put newspaper on the floor in front of the hearth and we had to kneel over the paper. She then combed our hair with a nit comb. As the nits dropped onto the newspaper, she used to 'crack' them with the comb. She felt ashamed that we had nits, although every other child at school had them as well. When she went down to the chemist in Nursery Road to get some nit shampoo, she waited outside until they opened, wearing a head scarf and dark glasses because she didn't want to be seen.

Anglesey Street school photo. My friend Sandra is standing up on the far left.

The school caretaker's house.

One day when I was at Infant school, we were marched down to Hunters Road as Princess Margaret was arriving in Birmingham and her route took her past the Carnegie Welfare Centre. We stood on the pavement and watched her go by in her big car. The day was somewhat spoilt for me though because I had been told off by a policeman for dropping fruit Spangles wrappers in the road and been made to pick them up. I was terrified that anyone would find out that I had been told off by a policeman.

I remember that on one edge of the playground were the old air raid shelters which were off limits but we would go and peek through the slightly open door to see what mysteries were inside. I was shy and did not want to disobey the teacher's edicts, unlike some daredevils who actually ventured inside. When we were in the juniors, my friend Sandra and I were asked if we would like to earn some pocket money by washing up the teachers' teacups in the staff room; we readily agreed. We used to go in when they weren't there and enjoyed snooping round the staff room. One of the teachers, Miss Dandy, was a tiny young woman who wore stiletto heels which she left in the staff room when she went to the classroom. Sandra and I used to love trying her shoes on and tottering around in them, good job we were never caught! The teachers used to give us three old pennies a week for our chores and we would go straight over to the corner shop opposite the school.

This was a grocery store run by a lady whose old deaf uncle used to help her in the shop. It was his job to serve the sweets and these were divided into the 'halfpenny tray', the 'penny tray' and so on until you reached the dizzy heights, sweet-wise of the 'threepenny tray'. They weren't trays but Oxo tins with various sweets in such as Sherbet Dabs, Flying Saucers and liquorice sweets. Uncle was profoundly deaf and we had to shout very loudly to get him to understand. His niece, if she was in the shop, would get irritated with him as it took an awful lot of shouting to get what we wanted. What a treat we had spending our three old pence on sweets and I think we ate them all ourselves, sharing was not a concept we had discovered at this stage in our development.

Later on in the Juniors, the school was actually too small to hold all of us so arrangements were made to build an 'annex', we had to move elsewhere to continue our education and so we went to rooms behind the Friends Meeting House in Farm Street, Hockley. Here, as well as our normal lessons, we used to have musicians from the City of Birmingham Orchestra come to play to us and teach us about music and musical instruments.

We must have been at Farm Street for at least a year and I sat my 11 plus there. Finally when the 'annex' was ready, we were all marched up from Farm Street to the official opening of the new building and I spent my last year at Junior school in one of the new classrooms. The only thing I can remember about this last year is that we had a fish tank in the classroom with maggots in so that we could watch them develop into flies. One of the boys threw a maggot down my dress and I was too scared to tell the teacher. It stayed there until I went home and went into the bathroom to change and it fell on the floor. I was so frightened that I spent the day in mental torture thinking I was going to be eaten alive (by the maggot not the teacher)!

One year, a few of us were gathered around the piano at school to try out some songs. This was actually an audition to see if we could sing in tune. Some of us could, so we joined a vast number of other school children at Birmingham Town Hall for a concert. We used to go for practices and on the evening of the concert, to be in such a prestigious venue and to be singing in front of our parents made us proud.

My friend at Junior school was Sandra who lived over the road from us. She was an only child and therefore seemed to have things which I would have loved to have. Her Mom worked in the Jewellery Quarter and for one birthday, Sandra gave me a gold locket. Her Mom also took us to the pictures and I remember at the age of nine or 10, she took us to see 'The Vikings' starring Tony Curtis and Kirk Douglas. It was a bit gruesome in parts, especially when an eagle took out the eye of Kirk Douglas, but we kept watching. Sandra also had ballet and tap lessons at a dance school and I was so envious. At the end of every term, the dance school put on a show which Sandra's mom took me to see. They had amazing costumes for the show and I desperately wanted to join the dance school but was not allowed to. Sandra also had a pony tail and I wanted to grow my hair but that also was out of the question.

Sandra's nan lived at the bottom of Villa Street in a large terraced house. Her back yard was paved with blue bricks and across the middle ran an open drainage channel which carried water used in the kitchen. Sandra and I used to take our shoes and socks off and paddle in this water pretending we were at the seaside. Next door lived an old lady who people said was a witch. We used to peek round the corner of the outhouse into her yard and if she saw us, we used to run.

I was made to have piano lessons which I did not want (no comparison with a dance school!). The piano was second hand with brass candlesticks which swung out from the front of the piano. The piano teacher, Mrs Hall who lived at the top of Mayfield Road used to teach me and Diane but I did not practice very much and eventually was allowed to give up. My cousin, Diane, also gave up and we both now wish we had paid a bit more attention. When I stopped piano lessons, Mom in her usual 'throwing out' mood, asked Dad to chop up the piano in the yard, he got so far with it but then discovered that it had an iron frame he could not chop through. I don't know how they got rid of it in the end, the last I saw of it, the frame was being wheeled down the entry.

I was very shy at school, my school report usually said that I knew the answers to questions but was too shy to put my hand up. One of the first teachers I had was Miss White, she looked old to us but was probably only in her forties. She had her hair plaited in two buns at the side of her head, they looked like earphones. She always wore the same dress, it seemed to me, it was grey worsted with diagonal white stripes. She was very strict and I was afraid of her and I think I got a slap on the legs once for either doing something I shouldn't or not doing something I should have. I was glad when I moved out of her class although she encouraged me in writing. I still have some of the stories I wrote in my textbook and she always marked them and put comments on them. I once wrote a story about a highwayman holding up a coach and her comment was 'a rattling good story Gillian'.

It was a proud moment for my parents in 1960 when I passed the 11 plus, one of five in my class. I got a place at King Edward's Grammar School for Girls, Handsworth. On the first day there, I went wearing a too big uniform that I 'would grow into' and the start of a life which would change with the advent of the 60s. The old fashioned days of the 40s and 50s were turned upside down and left behind, along with my childhood, in the excitement of a new decade – but that's another story!

Chapter 10

The Last Link

S o that's my story of Lozells and some of its inhabitants who were part of my history. Dad was amazing because he had had a heart attack at 60 and then retired from work. He was on medication for years and eventually was diagnosed with heart failure but he was always a very active man. At the age of 92, he had a pacemaker fitted. He then became even more active in what we call his 'gap year'. He went travelling on trains with his trusty

Dad on his 'gap year'.

backpack to places such as Liverpool, Manchester, Bristol and London as he enjoyed sightseeing; we never knew where he would call us from next!

The last link with Lozells ended in 2016 when my dad died at the age of 96 after living in Church Street, Lozells all his life. He was always well dressed, a dapper gentleman wearing a cravat, still driving his beloved old Fiesta, still building his model railway in the front room up to two weeks before he died. For the funeral, we had a little card made with the following words on by Richard Fife. And for me, these thoughts sum up not just Dad, but all of my Lozells family.

No person is ever truly alone
Those who live no more
Whom we loved
Echo still within our thoughts
Our words, our hearts
And what they did and who they were
Becomes a part of all that we are
Forever